THE RIGHT CONNECTION

(A Collection of Puppet Skits)

by *Iris Gray Dowling*

Iris Gray Dowling

John 3:16

Faithful Life Publishers
North Fort Myers, FL 33903

FaithfulLifePublishers.com

The Right Connection

Copyright © 2015 by Iris Gray Dowling
ISBN: 978-1-63073-086-4

Author and Editor in chief: Iris Gray Dowling

Assistant Editor: Elsie Peters Shepherd assisted in reading and editing the puppet skits.

Cover Picture: Robert Jordan Dowling

Iris Gray Dowling
163 Pusey Mill Road
Cochranville, PA 19355

Phone: 610-932-9699
~~irisgdow@juno.com~~
dowlingiris013@gmail.com

Published and printed by:
Faithful Life Publishers • North Fort Myers, FL 33903
888.720.0950 • info@FaithfulLifePublishers.com

Permission is granted to the purchaser of this book to make necessary copies in order to perform these skits in your church or club groups—not for resale. All other copying is prohibited without permission from the author or publisher.

Printed in the United States of America.

19 18 17 16 15   1 2 3 4 5

Free to all God's Helpers

Preface and Dedication

The purpose of this book is to provide puppet skits designed to help those working in children's ministries. A variety of topics has been used, including missions, patriotism, "Bible stories, holidays, and Biblical life principles. These three to eight minute skits can be enjoyed by preschool and early elementary age children and can be easily done by teens using ideas from the Introductory Pages.

This book is dedicated to my family (both biological and spiritual) with whom I have worked. They have provided a variety of character names and ideas. I thank the Lord for giving me sixty years of working in Children's Church, Vacation Bible Schools, Sunday school, and other ministries where I could be motivated by many boys and girls. They deserve credit for their willingness to work with me and use their talents in glorifying the Lord.

I thank the Lord that over the years He has put me in encouraging Southeastern Pennsylvania churches such as Bible Baptist Church, West Chester; East Goshen Bible Church, WC; Beulah Baptist Church, Oxford; and Highland Baptist Church, Parkesburg. In each of these I was encouraged to use my work for the furtherance of the Gospel.

It is my sincere hope and desire that those who use the puppet material compiled in this book and those who listen to the presentations will be equally blessed by its use. It is my prayer that the Gospel message presented in these puppet skits will reach boys and girls for Jesus Christ.

Yours in His service,

Iris Gray Dowling
Iris Gray Dowling
Philippians 4:13

"Shout with joy to God, all the earth! Sing the glory of His name; make His praise glorious!"

Introductory Notes and Ideas for Use of Puppets

Articles by this author attest to her belief in using drama to help teach the Bible to children. Included are some excerpts from her articles published in teaching magazines such as *Leader in Church School Today, Church Educator, Sunday School Leadership, Kids Ministry Ideas,* and *Resource*.

Many ideas from her articles to help in using a puppet ministry will be discussed in the following paragraphs. First, be sure to make a schedule for puppet programs so as not to become boring from overuse. Second, be sure to give puppeteers adequate time for preparation and not overload their busy schedules.

Since preschool children have short attention spans, puppets can provide effective activities to hold the interest of this age group. After the telling of a Bible story children can review by acting out the parts either with physical drama or with puppets. The class can make simple puppets to take home and continue to act out the story for family and friends. Early elementary students also enjoy making puppets with which they can retell the story, make applications, have question reviews, teach Bible verses, songs, and more.

Ideas for making <u>simple puppets</u> are as follows: use dolls with movable mouths, find animal puppets at yard sales, draw faces on your fisted hand, and make finger puppets from wide masking tape around the fingers. Other simple puppets can be made from tongue depressor sticks, lunch bags, socks, gloves, paper plates, forks, spoons, toilet paper rolls, clothes pins, craft sticks, styrofoam cups, meat trays, styrofoam balls (make a hole for the finger), upside down paint brush, upside down hand broom, corn husks, card/paper dolls, and plastic soap bottles. Draw the faces of the desired character and dress with cloth scraps. Velcro can be used to attach different costumes.

Puppet stages can vary from fancy to simple such as turning a table on its side, kneel behind a draped chair, put a spring rod across a doorway with a drape, or prop a large piece of cardboard against two chairs and raise the puppets above it. Make a stage by cutting a window in a large cardboard box, or Trifold Tabletop stage. A fancier stage can be made by joining PCV pipes and enclosed with curtains.

Older elementary children have a strong interest in drama activities. Middlers usually enjoy performing for others and being videotaped. They are very capable of writing and performing short skits that review Bible stories and Christian standards. The basic story ideas are written in these puppet skits. Clever puppeteers can add humorous conversation for the puppets without changing the story line or principles presented.

On the other hand, teens prefer working behind the scenes, but like being busy and involved. They make good puppeteers and script writers, as well as provide music, record sound effects, and adjust lighting and electronic equipment. Some can build stages and scenery or make puppets and puppet costumes, while others may prefer to be listeners and equipment managers.

A wise director provides opportunities for each person to work where he or she feels most comfortable. By working together, teens develop skills they didn't know they had. Involvement in a teen drama ministry with an adult supervisor can promote learning, growing, and serving the Lord.

Unequaled excitement comes from teaching with drama as we open new avenues of ministry for all ages.

* Refer to the *Appendixes* in the back for more puppet scripts by this author.

Table of Contents

Preface and Dedication 3

Introductory Notes and Ideas for Use of Puppets 5

1. **When the Door Is Closed** 11
   Jenna and Willie tell how God closed the ark door leaving unbelieving people outside when the flood came and how God will close heaven's door to those who refuse to believe on his Son. (Based on Genesis 7; Hebrews 11:7)

2. **When the Door is Opened** 18
   Jenna and Willie prepare to tell the second part of Noah's story after the storm. They show how God opens doors for us if we trust him. (Genesis 8 & 9)

3. **A Real Live Fish Story** 24
   The puppets tell the story of a miserable Jonah, who ran away from God and learned it was important to obey. (Based on Jonah 1--3)

4. **Never Alone** 30
   The puppets help kids realize Jesus cares about them and is with them everywhere they go when they know him as Savior.

5. **Who Is The Real Ruler?** 35
   Two siblings see how God deals with pride, even in the lives of kings (Based on Daniel 4 and Philippians 2:10, 11)

6. **The Fear Factor** 40
   Two kids decide to be more faithful to God after learning how God punished a proud ruler and rewarded his faithful servant, Daniel. (Based on Daniel 5)

7. **Who Is The Winner?** 45
   Debbie, who thinks she knows the Bible inside out, loses the Bible Quiz finals. Jen tries to help Debbie see she was too proud.

8. **How God Works In Exciting Ways** 50
   The puppets get upset over their mission bank being stolen, but learn how God works in spite of bad events. The puppets tell Daniel's story in Bible Club. (Based on Daniel 6)

9. **Inside Out** 57
   Mikie, who acts conceited because he can afford lots of nice clothes, doesn't want to play with kids who can't. His friend, Jenna helps him see he may look good on the outside, but needs changes on the inside. (Based on 1 Samuel 16:7)

10. **On The Rescue Team** 63
    Mikie thinks he can be a rescue worker without training. Ami tells him how he can be a rescuer of sin sick people. (Based on John 3:16)

11. **Who is Your Hero?** 70
    Mikie imitates his sports hero in the way he dresses and acts, but learns he should imitate someone much more important. (Based on Romans 6:23; 1 Peter 3:3-5)

12. **Lasting Forever** 77
    Mikie wants to get people to save the earth and its resources, but he learns it's important for people to know about God's plans.

13. **Ready For Heaven** 82
    Mikie, a shy boy, is afraid to have the kids look at him, but with the help of his sister, Amy, they talk about heaven and the importance of being ready to go there. (Based on Revelation 20:15; 21:27; John 14:1-6)

14. Born Blind 89
Benjie tells about his friend born physically blind. He learns that all people are born spiritually blind until they know Jesus as Savior. (Based on John 9)

15. A Robber Asks Forgiveness 96
A conversation on the forgiveness of Onesimus makes our puppets see the need to forgive and forgive again. (Based on Philemon 8, 21; Colossians 4:7-9)

16. The Surprise Sports Star 100
Dad arranged a surprise visit from a sports star. The visitor told the kids a story of a Biblical athlete, David. (1 Samuel 16)

17. A Good Tip 108
Ethan learns the importance of carrying God's Word in his heart. (Psalms 119: 2, 9--11, 105)

18. Falling Short 113
Every person falls short of God's standard. God's Son brought salvation and forgiveness of sins. Acceptance of these gifts helps us reach God's standard. (Based on Romans 3:22-24)

19. A Memory Poem (Patriotism) 119
The girls talk about how important it is to remember those who fought for our freedom and how we can show our appreciation.

20. Something Different to Surprise Dad 124
Jenna wants to make Dad's birthday memorable. She learned that working together with her siblings is best.

Appendixes..129
    Other Puppet Skits written by Iris Gray Dowling
    (Rights owned by others)

    Books containing Puppet Skits written by Iris Gray Dowling

Topical and Bible References Index 135
for using these Puppet Skits

Biography of Iris Gray Dowling 137

Other Books Written by Iris Gray Dowling 138

"When The Door Is Closed"   # 1.

SUMMARY: Jenna and Willie tell how God closed the ark's door leaving unbelieving people outside when the flood came and how God will close Heaven's door to those who refuse to believe on His Son.

CHARACTERS: *(Two puppets between 7 and 10 years old)*

    JENNA...*girl puppet nine years old*

    WILLIE...*boy puppet a year younger*

AT RISE: (*JENNA talks to kids in the class*).

JENNA: My friend came back today. Of course you know who I'm talking about. *(pause for answer--Willie)* Do you know why Willie wasn't here for so long? *(pause for answer)* He had a fever. His temperature wouldn't go down...and he coughed so much he got sick at his stomach. *(pause)* He's better now. I'll let him tell you the rest. *(pause)* It was kind of hard getting him to come today. *(pause)* Do you think you could be real quiet until he comes in the door? *(pause)* Then you could clap and act glad to see him. *(pause as **WILLIE** enters)*

KIDS: *(shout and clap hands)* Hurrah! Willie!

WILLIE: *(jumps back; acts scared)* Am I in the right place? Is this a church group?

The Right Connection by Iris Gray Dowling

JENNA: Yeah, Willie. Don't you like the way the boys and girls are happy to see you?

WILLIE: Oh, I forgot how excited kids can get. It's been so quiet at my house while I was sick.

JENNA: Willie, we're all glad you're back. You're feeling okay, aren't you?

WILLIE: I sure am glad I'm not coughing so much, but I still can't sing.

JENNA: That's all right. We won't ask you to sing.

WILLIE: *(frowns)* O. K. What do you want me to do then?

JENNA: Maybe you can help me tell a story.

WILLIE: Is it one I know. *(pause as he looks at her)* Tell me, why do you always get to prepare ahead of time, but I don't.

JENNA: I'm sure you know about Noah... *(pause)*

WILLIE: That's easy. Everybody knows about Noah and the ark, even these kids.

JENNA: Yes, I'm sure...But maybe we can tell them something they don't know.

WILLIE: What could that-a-a-t be?

JENNA: Let's start the story and we'll find out...okay?

WILLIE: May I start? (*looks at JENNA who shakes her head yes*) People acted real bad in Noah's day.

JENNA: (*interrupts*) ...sounds like people today (*pause*). You mean they were sinful?

WILLIE: Don't interrupt me! (*looks at JENNA with a frown; puts hand over her mouth; tries to tell more of the story quickly*) God wasn't pleased with those wicked people, so he sent a flood over the whole earth to drown them all...(*pause*) and that's the end of that story.

JENNA: No-o-o...it's not! You forgot there was one man who pleased God.

WILLIE: Yeah...Noah.

JENNA: And Noah's wife, their sons, and their wives also believed God.

WILLIE: But God didn't stop the flood for just those eight people.

JENNA: No, but he made a plan to save them from drowning.

WILLIE: Oh yeah...(*puts hand to head as thinking*) You're right! God told Noah to build a boat.

JENNA: Not just a boat...no one had ever seen such a humongous boat.

WILLIE: One that could hold a lot of people!

The Right Connection by Iris Gray Dowling

JENNA: Yes, God wanted people to repent. So he gave them about 100 years to change. Noah preached to them a long time, but no one, not a single one, repented.

WILLIE: It's hard to believe that no one believed Noah in 100 years of preaching, isn't it?

JENNA: Yep...they thought he was crazy for building such a gigantic boat...With only a little tiny river to float it in.

WILLIE: Well, isn't that logical?

JENNA: Willie, sometimes our friends think we're crazy when we do right things even when everyone else is doing wrong. They know it's because we're Christians, and they laugh at us like they laughed at Noah.

WILLIE: Funny, Noah acted like it didn't bother him. He kept on building. I don't think I could be as brave as Noah...

JENNA: That's right. The more the people laughed the harder he pounded. He showed us how to be determined to do what God wants.

WILLIE: You got that right!

JENNA: You know before Noah's day it had never rained on the earth.

WILLIE: (*looks at JENNA inquisitively*) You mean those people never saw one rainy day, let alone forty rainy days? No wonder they called Noah crazy!

JENNA: But Noah had faith and believed God, even if he hadn't seen rain.

WILLIE: Yep, that's faith all right. (*pause*) I wonder how he got those wild animals on that boat.

JENNA: In the Bible it says God sent them into the ark, two by two, male and female. Even the animals obeyed God.

WILLIE: Wow! That's something new I didn't hear before.

JENNA: (*points to verses and reads verses*) Look right here in Genesis, chapter 7, verses 9 and 15. It says Noah was inside as the animals came in.

WILLIE: That's awesome! If animals know enough to obey God, we should too.

JENNA: Good point, Willie. Once the animals were in the boat with Noah's family, the Bible says God shut the door.

WILLIE: (*looks inquiring*) Whoa! God shut the door?

JENNA: Yep, and no one could get it open from the outside or inside.

WILLIE: And all those mockers were locked out!

JENNA: Yes, Willie. Noah and his family felt safe.

WILLIE: But the ones outside weren't safe!

JENNA: No, God gave all those wicked people years to repent and turn to him, but they wouldn't! So when God shut Noah in, he shut them out.

WILLIE: That's sad. I wonder how Noah and his family felt when people started screaming, "Let us in! Let us in!"

JENNA: I'm sure they felt sad, but the people had gotten lots of warnings.

WILLIE: And they had lots of chances to believe, right?

JENNA: Many people today are just like that—they hear God's message of salvation over and over, but don't accept Jesus as their Savior. It will be sad when God closes Heaven's door leaving them out.

WILLIE: Right! People should believe and repent while they have a chance. Once this earthly life is over, their chance is gone.

JENNA: Right...people should believe and repent while they can.

WILLIE: That sounds sad. I don't want anyone to get locked out of Heaven.

JENNA: Those are wise words Willie. *(looks toward the boys and girls)* How about you boys and girls? Does anyone here want to believe and ask God to forgive your sins? (*Wait a minute. If any say Yes, have a teacher talk with them.*)

WILLIE: Is it time to go now?

JENNA: Yes, but if you boys and girls come back next week, we'll tell you the next part of the story and how God opened the door of that big boat.

WILLIE: Awesome! This time you'll let me get ready ahead of time, won't you? Bye, everybody.

BOTH: *(wave good-bye and exit)*

* * *

Suggested Bible References: Genesis 6, 7; John 3:16; Hebrews 11:7.

The Right Connection by Iris Gray Dowling

2. "When The Door Is Opened"

SUMMARY: Jenna and Willie prepare to tell the second part of Noah's story after the storm. They show how God opens doors for us if we trust him. (Based on Genesis 8 and 9:1-17)

CHARACTERS: *(two puppets aged 7 to 9 years old)*

    JENNA...*girl puppet nine years old*

    WILLIE...*boy puppet one year younger*

(***JENNA*** *and* ***WILLIE*** *enter hugging their toy animals*)

WILLIE: I'm ready to tell about Noah and the animals this time.

JENNA: Don't you need to start by having good manners?

WILLIE: What did I do wrong?

JENNA: You didn't even say, "good morning" to the kids.

WILLIE: Okay. (*says to* ***JENNA***) Good morning, Jenna. (*says to* ***KIDS***) Good morning, kids. (*looks oddly at* ***JENNA***)...but it wasn't such a good morning.

JENNA: What do you mean?

WILLIE: I heard about lots of floods in the news. It rained five inches in some places and many people drowned, almost like in Noah's day.

Page 18   *The Right Connection* by Iris Gray Dowling

JENNA: Not quite, but it is sad. That reminds us that we never know when things like that might happen and we need to be ready for heaven.

WILLIE: Yeah, you're right. That's not like people in Noah's day who weren't ready.

JENNA: Five inches is a lot of rain and causes local floods. But I know God will never destroy the whole earth by a flood again.

WILLIE: You can't really know that! These floods were pretty bad.

JENNA: I believe what God says in the Bible. God put a rainbow in the sky for all people to see, and said, "This is my promise that I won't destroy the whole earth again by a flood".

WILLIE: I'm glad about that.

JENNA: The Bible shows us that God kept his promises over and over.

WILLIE: The story is over and I didn't get to tell some parts of Noah's story.

JENNA: Really? Go ahead. You can tell the parts we missed.

WILLIE: After the forty days of rain Noah stayed in the ark many months with all those animals.

JENNA: Yeah, that's right.

The Right Connection by Iris Gray Dowling

WILLIE: Don't interrupt! (*looks at her*) God sent a wind to help dry up some of the water. After 150 days the ark stopped on Mt. Ararat. Ten months later Noah sent some doves out of the window.

JENNA: You sure covered a lot of time, but it really must have gone slow in the ark. There were seven days between the times he sent out each of the birds.

WILLIE: Okay, the birds helped. Noah didn't know the waters were drying up a little when the first dove came back with nothing.

JENNA: Yes, but the second dove came back with a live branch in its bill.

WILLIE: And the third bird didn't come back at all...

JENNA: But Noah didn't come out of the ark until God opened the door just like he closed it—from the outside. Now you tell what happened next.

WILLIE: Okay. Don't rush me.

JENNA: Well, this was when the rush began.

WILLIE: You mean the parade began. That must have been a sight to see. (*holds hand up to his eyes as if looking in the distance*)

JENNA: Then God told them all to replenish the earth.

WILLIE: That means every family got bigger.

JENNA: Noah didn't forget God. He built an altar and thanked God for the blessings and care for his family in the ark.

WILLIE: He thanked God for a flood?

JENNA: Can't you see God helped Noah prepare ahead of time for the flood? Noah believed God would send the flood, just like He said.

WILLIE: Oh, I get it. Noah believed God would keep him safe through the flood.

JENNA: You got it. It takes faith to believe God will keep His promises when we're going through a bad time.

WILLIE: I'm glad I learned so much more about God today. He IS in charge of everything.

JENNA: Just one thing—he leaves us in charge of making decisions to believe or not to believe. He closes doors and opens doors just like he did with Noah.

WILLIE: I guess you are right about that. First, we have to choose to open our heart's door to God. Then we can trust Him to help us make the right decisions.

JENNA: In Noah's day, most of the people didn't choose to believe what God said. There are people like that today. They don't believe what the Bible says.

WILLIE: Some people think the Bible is just another book of literature or history.

JENNA: But we know from the Bible that God is involved in people's lives. He had plans for Noah and his family and he has plans for each one of us if we trust him.

WILLIE: After what I learned I'm always going to trust God to help me make decisions.

JENNA: Me too. I don't know how people live without God in their lives.

WILLIE: Wow! I never thought of that. Now I can know God IS in control. (*yawns*)

JENNA: You look like you're getting tired.

WILLIE: A little, but I know I can take a nap and wake up where God plans for me to be.

JENNA: We need to tell the boys and girls more about God so they can be sure of knowing him and trusting His wise plans for them.

WILLIE: Okay, but can we do that next time since I'm really getting tired?

JENNA: Yes, maybe that would be better. God will help us get ready and do a better job.

WILLIE: Isn't it time to go home now?

JENNA: Yes. Why don't you say good-bye? I'm glad you could make it today, Willie.

The Right Connection by Iris Gray Dowling

WILLIE: See you next time, boys and girls. (***WILLIE*** *waves and exits*)

JENNA: *(pause* to *hear **WILLIE** snoring back stage)* It sounds like he's already asleep. Maybe we can sing a few songs while we wait for Mr. Sleepy Head to wake up. Can we try? *(say title of a song to fit the theme of trusting in God). (Suggested Songs: "Countdown"; "I Have Decided to Follow Jesus"; "Trust and Obey".)*

* * *

#3. "A Real Live Fish Story"

THEME: Obedience.

SUMMARY: The puppets tell the story of a disobedient Jonah, who ran away from God and how God taught him to obey. Based on Jonah 1-3

CHARACTERS: (*performed with two puppets aged seven to ten*)

    SARA......*older girl puppet*

    ROBBIE.....*younger boy puppet*

SARA: Hey, Robbie. We have a neat story to tell the kids today.

ROBBIE: I've got a cool story, too. When will you let me tell mine?

SARA: Let's do this Bible story first.

ROBBIE: Then I'll tell my story!

SARA: You know Jonah. (*pause;* ***ROBBIE*** *nods yes*) He had a big problem. He disobeyed God.

ROBBIE: I thought he got on a ship to take a trip.

SARA: He did, but the Bible says God told him to preach to Nineveh's wicked people so they would repent of their sins, and he didn't want to do it.

ROBBIE: I guess he was afraid.

SARA: He didn't think the people would repent and maybe they'd make fun of him. So he got into a ship sailing the opposite direction from Nineveh.

ROBBIE: Didn't he know God could see him wherever he went?

SARA: I guess he knew, but tried to forget about it. He thought he couldn't see God if he went to sleep in a dark room down in the bottom of the ship.

ROBBIE: But God saw him down there and sent a horrible storm... *(pause; laughing)* that blew him straight to Nineveh.

SARA: Not that fast! God didn't joke around. He did send a bad storm! It really scared the sailors. They were afraid of sinking.

ROBBIE: *(smiles)* Humm...I guess old Jonah wasn't scared.

SARA: No, he slept through it all--the worst storm those scared sailors ever experienced. They knew right away God was angry, but they didn't know why.

ROBBIE: Then they threw Jonah off the ship so a big fish could swallow him.

SARA: Slow down. The sailors tried everything to keep the ship floating, even praying to their false gods.

ROBBIE: Well it didn't help, did it?

The Right Connection by Iris Gray Dowling

SARA: No, so they woke Jonah. He admitted his God was angry with his disobedience. He told them the storm wouldn't stop until he was off the ship.

ROBBIE: So they threw him overboard.

SARA: They didn't want to. Jonah told them they had to, or they'd sink.

ROBBIE: That was kind of him. But he must have known he wouldn't live.

SARA: Yeah, That's when God sent a big fish to swallow Jonah.

ROBBIE: Oh, he continued his nap in the fish's belly?

SARA: More like being on a roller coaster ride.

ROBBIE: Wow! You mean he rode a roller coaster for three days and three nights?

SARA: It wasn't much fun with decayed seaweeds wrapped around his head and body.

ROBBIE: Oh...gross!

SARA: And he felt like he was burning.

ROBBIE: Burning? *(pause)* Like fire?

SARA: The fish's stomach had digestive acids that felt like fire and chemicals burning him.

ROBBIE: Wow! That's worse than drowning.

SARA: But God didn't plan to let him die. Next Jonah prayed.

ROBBIE: To the God he was running from?

SARA: He knew things wouldn't get better if he didn't.

ROBBIE: Did God answer him?

SARA: God was there all the time. He made the fish get sick and it threw Jonah up on the beach.

ROBBIE: Yuk!

SARA: Yuk, is right! Jonah felt sick, too--lying in a pile of seaweed and throw up.

ROBBIE: Yuk! Yuk!

SARA: You see God was teaching Jonah that he should willingly obey Him.

ROBBIE: So he got up and went straight to Nineveh.

SARA: Yes, and he preached about their sins and got a big surprise!

ROBBIE: What could be worse than sea sickness and burning?

SARA: The people repented.

ROBBIE: Oh-h-h! That's just what God wanted.

SARA: You're right. (*pause*) You know sometimes we don't obey God like we should.

ROBBIE: But He doesn't send a fish to swallow us up.

SARA: But He can send unpleasant things to help us decide to obey.

ROBBIE: You think he really does that?

SARA: He could. He doesn't make us obey like we're puppets. He tries to help us see His way is best.

ROBBIE: I guess Jonah did learn God's way was best.

SARA: It's too bad he had to learn it the hard way.

ROBBIE: My Dad says that to me sometimes when I'm disobedient.

SARA: Yes, Robbie, we all act like that sometimes. (*pauses*)

ROBBIE: I think I'll try to be obedient to God after hearing this story.

SARA: Me, too, Robbie. (*pauses*) How about you boys and girls? Do you think it's important to obey God? He loves you and wants you to be willing to follow Him and obey His commands. (*pause for children's responses*) Wow! I think it's time for us to go now.

ROBBIE: Boy, time does fly by.

SARA: Really? I didn't see it.

ROBBIE: You don't want me to tell the moron joke do you?

SARA: I knew that's what you wanted to do.

ROBBIE: O.K. Time flew when he threw the clock out the window.

SARA: O.K. Time flew so we have to fly away too.

ROBBIE: Bye, boys and girls. I have to go look for my clock.

* * *

(*Now the children could sing some of these suggested songs: "Trust and Obey"; "OBEDIENCE"; "Listening, Listening"; "I'm Gonna Work"; "I Have Decided".*)

#4. "Never Alone"

SUMMARY: The puppets help kids realize Jesus cares about them and is with them everywhere they go when they know Him as Savior.

CHARACTERS: *(two puppets from ages 7 to 10)*

    ALLIE......*the older girl puppet*

    ROBBIE.....*the younger puppet*

PROPS: *Teddy bear.*

My Teddy Bear

ALLIE: Hi, Robbie. Hi, boys and girls.

ROBBIE: Hi, Allie. (*He waves his hand and hugs his toy bear tightly.*)

ALLIE: Robbie, you didn't name that bear after me, did you?

ROBBIE: No, I just like him more than any other toy, and more than I like you.

ALLIE: You should have left him home today.

ROBBIE: I love my Teddy bear and I want to keep him with me all the time.*(squeezes bear)*

Page 30   *The Right Connection* by Iris Gray Dowling

ALLIE: You love your bear that much?

ROBBIE: Sure do, and I'm taking him wherever I go.

ALLIE: That's all right, Robbie, but...

ROBBIE: But what?

ALLIE: Suppose you forget and leave him somewhere? Someone else might take him. Then you'd be upset!

ROBBIE: No, I won't do that. I'll hold onto him all the time.

ALLIE: How about when we go out to eat? Your hands are busy with the food.

ROBBIE: No-o problem.

ALLIE: You can't eat with both hands and hold the bear at the same time.

ROBBIE: (*pause*) Well, I will hold him in my lap with one hand.

ALLIE: You know, Robbie, Jesus wants us to love him so much that we want to stay close to him all the time like that.

ROBBIE: You mean that, don't you?

ALLIE: He holds us in his hand and he wants us to know he cares about us everywhere we go.

ROBBIE: If I'm in his hand I won't be able to go anywhere else.

The Right Connection by Iris Gray Dowling

ALLIE: He has you in his hand to protect you, but you are still free to go where you want.

ROBBIE: I'm not sure I understand that.

ALLIE: Jesus wants us to think about the places we go. If we can't take him with us, we'd better not go there.

ROBBIE: But he's living in me?

ALLIE: That's just it. We shouldn't go where Jesus would not go.

ROBBIE: You mean I should think, "Can I take Jesus with me?"

ALLIE: Now you've got it, Robbie.

ROBBIE: I don't want to hurt Jesus. (*raises both hands; let's bear fall*)

ALLIE: (*gets bear from the floor; hands bear to **ROBBIE***) Here's your bear.

ROBBIE: I guess I forgot about him for a minute.

ALLIE: I guess you did.

ROBBIE: But now, I get what you're saying.

ALLIE: Are you sure? (*pause*) There's always some kid watching us. We don't want to be a bad example for them either.

ROBBIE: You mean some kids might follow me if I do wrong. So I don't want to act like I forget Jesus is close to me.

ALLIE: That's true, Robbie.

ROBBIE: *(feels his lap for the bear; gets excited.)* Where's my bear?

ALLIE: You said you wouldn't forget your Teddy Bear because he's so important to you.

ROBBIE: I didn't forget. I just wanted to make sure he was near me.

ALLIE: Just like Jesus wants us to remember to stay close to him.

ROBBIE: I'm glad he cares so much about me.

ALLIE: Yeah, Jesus wants to be as important to us as we are to him.

ROBBIE: Oh, he wants me to remember what pleases him, right? *(pause)* I do want to do that.

ALLIE: Good, Robbie. We all should care about pleasing Jesus every day and every night.

ROBBIE: I think I'll leave my bear at home from now on, but I'll take Jesus with me wherever I go.

ALLIE: I'm sure Jesus is happy that you've made that choice.

ROBBIE: *(yawns noisily)*

ALLIE: You look a little tired, Robbie. *(pause)* I thought we were going to sing for the boys and girls.

The Right Connection by Iris Gray Dowling

ROBBIE: I'll try not to yawn.

ALLIE: O.K. let's try. You know "Keep Jesus First" [1], don't you?

ROBBIE: Oh, yeah (***ROBBIE*** *starts singing:* [1]*"Keep Jesus First" or other song that fits the theme. He yawns on the last words and stretches out the yawn*) "Keep Jesus first..fer..r..st..t...!"

ALLIE: Come on, let's set a better example for these kids.

ROBBIE: O.K. Let's sing.   (***BOTH*** *sing the song together*) (*pause; yawning*) I can't stop yawning. May I go home now?

ALLIE: O.K. You deserve a rest.

ROBBIE: Bye, boys and girls. (***BOTH PUPPETS*** *exit*)

*   *   *

[1] "Keep Jesus First" found in *Salvation Songs #3*, p. 23. <u>Child Evangelism.</u>

"Who Is The Real Ruler?" # 5.

THEME: Pride *(Based on Daniel 4 and Philippians 2:10,11)*

SUMMARY: Two siblings see how God deals with pride even in kings.

CHARACTERS: *(Two puppet siblings six to nine years old)*

    ROBIN.....*younger of the two puppets*

    CHRIS.....*a sibling two years older*

PROPS: *History books, map of Babylonian Empire.*

ROBIN: *(enters with his History book; looking puzzled)* This is so unbelievable!

CHRIS: *(enters; tries to look into **ROBIN**'s eyes)* You look like you just got bad news.

ROBIN: We studied about the Babylonian Empire in history class today. Wasn't Nebuchadnezzar one of the kings in the Bible during Daniel's life?

CHRIS: He was! You know, the Bible is a history book, too. The Bible says Nebuchadnezzar conquered Jerusalem and took the best young Jewish men to work in his court. Remember? Daniel was one of them.

ROBIN: Our teacher said Nebuchadnezzar controlled most of the world. Did he really?

The Right Connection by Iris Gray Dowling

CHRIS: Yep. And he was proud of himself because he'd conquered so much. (*pause; points to the book*) Look at this map. See how much land he ruled.

ROBIN: My teacher said he planned on ruling the whole world.

CHRIS: It's for sure that Nebuchadnezzar bragged all over his kingdom that he got the great Babylonian Empire by his own strength and power.

ROBIN: I guess he wanted lots of praise and honor from his people.

CHRIS: The Bible says God is not happy when people act proud and brag they can do everything without him.

ROBIN: We've studied about a lot of proud rulers in our history lessons.

CHRIS: Sure, but the Bible let's us in on a little secret about one of them. It tells how God taught King Nebuchadnezzar a lesson in humility.

ROBIN: Now I'm curious, where did you read that?

CHRIS: It's in God's History Book—the Bible. Daniel, chapter 4 tells about Nebuchadnezzar's dream. The odd thing was he knew the Most High God sent the dream, even though he wasn't a believer in the Almighty God of Heaven.

ROBIN: That's weird! How could you believe somebody sent something if you don't believe they exist?

CHRIS: It seems he had been watching Daniel and his friends after the fiery furnace ordeal. He was learning their God did exist.

ROBIN: So I guess he asked Daniel to tell him what the dream meant?

CHRIS: Sure did! Daniel told him the truth from God, even though that wasn't what the king wanted to hear.

ROBIN: Well, what was this terrible truth?

CHRIS: The dream predicted Nebuchadnezzar would go insane and live in fields like a wild animal.

ROBIN: Not the mighty ruler, Nebuchadnezzar!

CHRIS: Yes, the proud and mighty Nebuchadnezzar wasn't mightier than the King of Heaven who even rules in the kingdoms of men.

ROBIN: And it happened?

CHRIS: You said it! The dream predicted that he would crawl on the ground in a field and chew grass like an ox for seven years. And that's just what happened!

ROBIN: He actually crawled around in a meadow like an animal for seven years? How humbling for a great king!

CHRIS: He ate grass like an ox. His hair grew long and his nails grew like eagle claws.

ROBIN: Oh, gross!

CHRIS: Daniel also says in chapter four that Nebuchadnezzar finally lost his pride and lifted his eyes to give praise and honor to the King of Heaven.

ROBIN: That's good. *(points to head--thinking)* You know, there's a boy in my neighborhood who brags all the time. He says he's the smartest boy in school. He says no one knows all the things he knows. He interrupts the teacher constantly.

CHRIS: He should be careful about his bragging. He needs to realize God gave him his ability and God can also take it away.

ROBIN: How?

CHRIS: Sickness, accident, or just a simple mental problem like Nebuchadnezzar. God knows the best way to teach a humbling lesson to any proud person.

ROBIN: Yeah, I remember when one of America's leaders made an unwise statement. It caused a lot of people to get angry and demand that he resign his job. He had that very secure job for years, but lost it very quickly.

CHRIS: Things can change quickly, especially if God has a reason for the change.

ROBIN: History is really an interesting subject when you realize God has a part in the lives of powerful kings, who don't even believe in him.

CHRIS: I guess that's why Mom and Dad said we need to pray for our leaders. All people, even presidents, need God's wisdom and help each day.

ROBIN: It sure makes me realize how God does have a hand in people's lives, even though some refuse to believe it.

CHRIS: That's what the Bible teaches us.

ROBIN: That story about Nebuchadnezzar's pride has really made me think. I need to go home now and ask God to help me be more humble myself. (***ROBIN*** *exits yawning*)

CHRIS: God also wants all of us to practice being humble. See you next week, boys and girls. (***CHRIS*** *exits*)

ANNOUNCER: Nebuchadnezzar had to bow before God even if he didn't want to. So will everyone else who has ever lived on earth. They will have to bow and acknowledge that Jesus is Lord as it says in Philippians 2:10,11. (*Reads verses*) "That at the name of Jesus every knee should bow, of things in heaven and things in earth, and things under the earth; And that every tongue should confess that Jesus Christ is Lord, to the glory of God the Father."

BOTH PUPPETS: *(appear quickly to speak and leave when finished)* Wow! All kings, presidents, and every ordinary person will have to be humble before God even if they don't want to.

* * *

6. "The Fear Factor"

SUMMARY: Two kids decide to be more faithful to God after learning how God punished a proud ruler and rewarded his faithful servant, Daniel. (See Daniel 5)

CHARACTERS: *(two puppets 6 to 10 years old)*

    ROBIN......*a puppet 6 to 8 years old*

    CHRIS...... *a puppet a year older*

AT RISE: *Two puppet children continue studying History.*

CHRIS: I see you're studying that History book again.

ROBIN: After our talk about King Nebuchadnezzar, I'll never forget how powerful God is in the lives of rulers.

CHRIS: One reason we study history is so we can learn lessons from the past. I've learned God has everything under his control, even wicked kings.

ROBIN: Say, wasn't there another king in Daniel's time who was a little arrogant toward God?

CHRIS: Yeah, Daniel wrote about a Babylonian king that saw God's finger write a message on the wall.

ROBIN: Who was the message for?

CHRIS: Belshazzar, who was Nebuchadnezzar's grandson.

ROBIN: Why was God interested in writing a message to him?

CHRIS: When his grandfather, Nebuchadnezzar, captured Jerusalem, he took goblets from God's holy temple. Belshazzar got them out and used them to have a wild party.

ROBIN: Did he gobble down food out of the goblets?

CHRIS: Don't be silly. Goblets are delicate cups.

ROBIN: I'm sorry. I know they were sacred goblets used by the priests in God's temple.

CHRIS: Things in God's house were not meant to be played with.

ROBIN: How did Belshazzar play with them?

CHRIS: He praised false gods of silver and gold while he drank from God's holy goblets. He should have known better after what happened to his grandfather. He was a spoiled and rebellious king who gave no thought about Almighty God.

ROBIN: When he saw a finger write on the wall, I guess he didn't feel so rebellious and mighty.

CHRIS: No, he was so scared! He turned pale. His knees shook so bad his hips got out of joint.

ROBIN: Boy, that's really being scared! Did he fall down?

The Right Connection by Iris Gray Dowling

CHRIS: You better believe it! He knew the writing meant something serious.

ROBIN: So how did he find out what the message meant?

CHRIS: Of course he called his magicians and wise men. When they saw him they got the shock of their lives. They thought he was a ghost who had lost its balance.

ROBIN: So the answer got scared right out of them?

CHRIS: No, they didn't know the answer anyway. They just stared at the king on the floor shaking worse than a scared rabbit and looking very ghostly.

ROBIN: Why didn't Daniel come? I'm sure he knew the answer.

CHRIS: He wasn't close to this king, but the queen mother remembered Daniel and his great ability to interpret dreams. She advised her son to calm down and call Daniel.

ROBIN: Do you think Daniel hurried to the king when he called?

CHRIS: I'm sure he took time to pray and seek God's wisdom first. Daniel was a serious guy, you know. King Belshazzar promised him great rewards if he could tell the meaning of the writings.

ROBIN: Wow! He had a chance to become rich.

CHRIS: But Daniel wasn't after riches. His greatest desire was to please God.

ROBIN: That figures. (*pause*) Well, did he explain the meaning of the writing on the wall?

CHRIS: Sure...he said God was in charge of all kingdoms. He was going to end the Babylonian kingdom because of Belshazzar's rebellion toward God. The writing said the Medes and Persians would take Belshazzar's kingdom, divide it, and kill him.

ROBIN: That's just what my history teacher said happened. She told us the next world empire was the Medo-Persians. (*pause; looks at book*) Say, did the king live long enough to give Daniel the rewards he promised him?

CHRIS: Oh, yes. Belshazzar gave Daniel a purple robe, a gold chain, and the rule over one-third of his kingdom.

ROBIN: How long did that last?

CHRIS: The Medes came that night, slew Belshazzar, and took everything.

ROBIN: So Daniel didn't get to enjoy his rewards too long, did he?

CHRIS: Don't worry. God looked after Daniel. The new king made Daniel one of three presidents in his kingdom.

ROBIN: Oh, so God didn't forget his faithful follower?

CHRIS: No, and he won't forget us if we are faithful.

ROBIN: Our world today is a lot like Babylon. If Daniel could be loyal to God in such an evil country with rulers who dishonored God, so can we.

The Right Connection by Iris Gray Dowling

CHRIS: There are some world leaders in modern history who act like Belshazzar. Some still try to control people with tyranny and evil. And others set evil examples that influence the morals of our country.

ROBIN: I'm glad we had this discussion. At least I've learned that God still has everything under his control, even when it doesn't look like it.

CHRIS: He will let wicked and proud men rule for a while, but when it's the right time he'll bring them down and put someone else in their place.

ROBIN: And he'll never forget his loyal, faithful servants.

CHRIS: I want to be faithful like Daniel.

ROBIN: Maybe we can't take a stand for God before rulers, but we can stand against wrong in our schools and communities.

CHRIS: I'm not going to be too afraid to pray in front of my friends. I don't care what they think. I'll try to be loyal to God like Daniel.

ROBIN: From now on I'm going to attend the prayer time at the flag pole and thank God for my food at lunch.

CHRIS: Daniel prayed for God's wisdom three times a day. We should pray for God's wisdom every day too.

ROBIN: Let's sing * "Dare To Be a Daniel" because it takes courage to take a stand for God.

* (This song can be found in *Living Hymns*, Encore Publications. page 635.

"Who's The Winner?"   # 7.

SUMMARY: Debbie, who thinks she knows the Bible inside out, loses the Bible Quiz finals. Jen tries to help Debbie see she was too proud.

CHARACTERS: *(two sister puppets)*

    DEB...... *a young teen girl puppet*

    JEN...... *a girl puppet, Deb's sister*

    SCENE 1 -- *takes place <u>before</u> going to the Bible Quiz finals.*
    (Puppets enter)

DEB: Jen, I'm going to the Bible Quiz finals tonight; how about you?

JEN: *(happy tone)* Of course. I wouldn't miss cheering for my friends.

DEB: *(proud tone)* What about me? You know I'm going to win!

JEN: You should review your quiz answers a little, Debbie.

DEB: What's there to review? I won all the practices, so I won't have trouble winning tonight.

JEN: I hope you remember everything you think you know and they don't give you any surprise questions.

The Right Connection by Iris Gray Dowling

DEB: *(proud)* Don't worry. I know I'm good. *(pause; turns toward JEN)* Jen, why don't you make us both a sandwich before we go-o-o …. cause I don't want to be late.

JEN: *(sighs; looks away.)*

DEB: Don't you think I'll win?

JEN: *(shakes head)* I'm just glad I'm not one of the judges. (***JEN** exits*)

DEB: *(sarcastically; turns head toward **JEN**)* So am I! (***DEB** exits during Transition Music*)

SCENE 2 -- *takes place after the Bible Quiz finals.*

(***DEB** enters looking down.*)

JEN: *(enters)* You look a bit upset, Deb. *(shakes her head)* What happened to all your friends?

DEB: *(pouting)* Jill's getting all the attention I should get.

JEN: Why do you say that, Debbie? She won fair and square.

DEB: *(upset tone)* I lost the Bible Quiz finals to a girl who's only been a Christian one year. I can't believe she did so well.

JEN: Oh...you lost to someone you thought didn't know as much as you.

DEB: *(proudly)* Well, I am smarter. I've been winning every practice and now when they decide who's going to the finals, she won.

JEN: She may have studied a lot.

DEB: Didn't you hear? The judges gave her easier questions.

JEN: Oh, I don't think that's true.

DEB: *(sharply)* Of course, you wouldn't. You're not the one who lost to her.

JEN: No, I wasn't in the contest, but I heard all the questions and answers.

DEB: *(sarcastic)* So did I!

JEN: But you were concentrating mostly on your own answers. Since I wasn't a contestant, I'm in a better position to know if the judges were fair.

DEB: *(nasty)* I don't care what you think. They weren't fair!

JEN: Have it your way. I have to study for a test tomorrow. I can't pass without studying.

DEB: Is that a dig? I told you I didn't have to study. I know the Bible inside out.

JEN: Maybe that's part of your problem. You let your pride get in the way.

The Right Connection by Iris Gray Dowling

DEB: I really don't want to talk about it anymore!

JEN: Okay, but you should have asked for God's help before the quizzes.

DEB: Well, I forgot.

MOM: Mom told you yesterday to get ready spiritually. Didn't you know what she meant?

DEB: I thought she meant study the Bible more.

JEN: It seems you didn't even meet God half way.

DEB: *(meeker)* I guess I didn't.

JEN: Sometimes God needs to teach us lessons about winning or losing.

DEB: What do you mean?

JEN: Not to think you know it all without studying.

DEB: Well, I won all the practices.

JEN: Maybe that's why God had to change your prideful attitude. It was like a test, you know.

DEB: *(pause)* I guess you're saying I should study even if I know the answers?

Page 48   *The Right Connection* by Iris Gray Dowling

JEN: You still don't get it, do you? It's good to be confident, but not proud. God makes it clear in the Bible that He doesn't like pride, but I know you know that!

DEB: Do you think that is why I lost?

JEN: I'm not God, but maybe you ought to read what God says about pride.

DEB: I guess there <u>is</u> more in the Bible for me to learn.

JEN: Mom and Dad said there is always more in the Bible to learn. You know, God will help us when we realize we need His help. When we don't think we need His help, sometimes He let's us do it our way, so we can learn a good lesson.

DEB: (*meekly*) Maybe I was too confident.

JEN: You could talk to God about your pride. You can ask Him to help you be more humble. (*pause*) I'm going to bed. I have a hard schedule at school tomorrow. (*pause; **JEN** exits.*)

DEB: I think I'll stay here and read a few minutes. *(She reads her Bible; looks up enlightened; folds hands in prayer.)* Dear Lord. Forgive me for thinking I was so smart. Help me ask for your help in the future. Thanks for teaching me what I needed. Amen. (**DEB** *puts her head down, then slides from view during final music-- "Nothing Between".*)

* * *

The Right Connection by Iris Gray Dowling

#8. "How God Works In Exciting Ways"

THEME: Believe in God's Power (Based on Daniel 6)

SUMMARY: The puppets get upset over their mission bank being stolen but learn to see how God works in spite of bad events. The puppets tell Daniel's story in Bible Club.

CHARACTERS: (*two children puppets and one woman puppet***)**

> **ZANE...** *a boy puppet*
>
> **ALLIE...** *a girl puppet*
>
> **MOM...** *an older puppet--the children's mother*
>
> **SCENE 1:** *beginning with **ZANE** and **ALLIE** discussing a problem.*

ZANE: *(excited):* Something awful happened!

ALLIE: What, Zane?

ZANE: *(fretting)* Somebody took our Bible Club mission bank. It's not on our secret shelf.

ALLIE: Are you sure? Who would take it?

ZANE: I don't know, but it's gone.

ALLIE: (*fretting*): We worked so hard for that money. I cleaned the dishes a hundred nights to earn my part.

ZANE: I worked hard, too. I helped Dad with yard work every week.

ALLIE: Now some of our missionary friends can't buy Bibles for kids who don't have one.

ZANE: I can't believe someone would take our money.

MOM: (*enters*) Did I hear you say your mission bank is gone? You know, it really wasn't your money.

ZANE: What do you mean? Whose was it?

MOM: It was God's money. You collected it for His work. Maybe He has plans to use it another way.

ZANE: I don't understand what you're saying.

MOM: We don't always understand God's ways. You see, children, God knows who took the money.

ZANE: Why would he let someone do that?

MOM: We can't always know what God's plans are or how he works in another person's life. We need to pray for that person.

ALLIE: Isn't it time for us to go to Bible Club at Emily's house?

MOM: You will have to think about a new plan.

The Right Connection by Iris Gray Dowling

ZANE: Why plan when we don't have any money?

MOM: All we had and ever will have is the Lord's. He knows where the money is. We have to let him use it in his way.

ZANE: I know you're right, Mom, but it's so hard to understand.

ALLIE: *(puzzled)* I don't feel like earning more money for people to steal!

MOM: Remember, God knows all about it. Keep praying and trusting him.

(Suggested Transition Music: "Why Worry When You Can Pray".)

SCENE 2: *Puppets at Bible Club—tell the story of Daniel (in Daniel 6)*

ZANE: Boys and girls, our friend Daniel had been promoted to First President in the land of Persia. He still trusted God and prayed every day--morning, noon, and night.

ALLIE: He was not ashamed to pray at his window that faced Jerusalem where the people in the land of Persia could see him.

ZANE: Why did he do that?

ALLIE: He loved God and wanted to show he was serious about worshipping his God. There were some jealous people who didn't like it that Daniel was made a ruler.

ZANE: Some people were jealous of King Darius' devotion to Daniel. They set a trap to get rid of him.

ALLIE: I remember, they asked the king slyly, "Why don't you make a decree for thirty days. No one is to consult any other God or man, but you. If they do they'll be put in the lions' den."

ZANE: That didn't stop Daniel. He still prayed at his open window three times a day.

ALLIE: Those jealous people thought they had tricked Daniel. They knew he'd keep praying.

ZANE: So of course, they saw Daniel praying and reported it to the king. Darius was upset because he loved Daniel. He tried to think of a way to change his decree, but it was sealed with his seal and it had to be obeyed.

ALLIE: Sadly the king had to carry out his ruling and punish Daniel. Of course, the jealous men were happy to put Daniel into the lions' den with hungry lions.

ZANE: You all know how God shut the lions' mouths all night. Daniel came out without a scratch.

ALLIE: The king had a restless, sleepless night. He jumped up early in the morning and quickly went to the lions' den. He called to Daniel, "Has your God taken care of you?"

ZANE: He was relieved to find Daniel was not even scratched. He told the whole kingdom about Daniel's God being the true and living God.

ALLIE: Next, the king threw Daniel's enemies into the den of lions. oooouh!

ZANE: Oo-oo-ooh. The li-ons were hun-gr-y!

ALLIE: You bet they were! And they had a BIG dinner.

ZANE: Kids, before we leave we have to remind you that someone took the money we've all been saving to buy Bibles for kids who don't have one.

ALLIE: I learned from Daniel's story that God can turn the bad happenings around if we pray and trust him.

ZANE: Yes, you're right. Let's pray before we go. "Dear Lord, Don't let the robber spend your money. Bring it back so we can use it for the Bibles."

Transition Music as the puppets exit: "Dare to Be a Daniel".

SCENE 3: (*Kid puppets enter first, followed by Mom.*)

MOM: *(happily)* It was a week ago that Bible Club met and you prayed. Look what I found in our mailbox.

ZANE: (*sees bank; lean forward to look*) Somebody sent the mission bank back?

ALLIE: What about our money?

MOM: It's all here with a note.

ALLIE: A note? What does it says?

MOM: I'll read it to you. (*pauses;* **MOM** *reads note.*) "I knew I should not take the bank. I knew what you saved the money for, so I couldn't spend it. I had to return it."

ALLIE: How can we let this person know we're thankful?

MOM: I'm sure he knows. God seems to be working in his heart.

ZANE: (*amazed*) Isn't it exciting to see how God works?

MOM: We can count on our God. (*pauses; knock, knock is heard.*) Would you answer the door, Zane?

ZANE: (*pause as Zane exits a moment*) It's the kids from the neighborhood.

ALLIE: Why did they come today?

ZANE: They heard about the stolen money and brought their savings to put in the fund to buy Bibles. (*shows the money*)

ALLIE: (*delighted*) We didn't expect this!

ZANE: Awesome! Now we have three times as much money as we had before.

ALLIE: God is full of surprises, isn't he? He really answered our prayers in a BIG way!

MOM: I'm sure God's work is not finished yet. Remember what we said last week? It's important to keep praying for the person who took the bank.

ZANE: We will, Mom. But let's send this money to our missionaries to buy the Bibles before somebody else takes it.

MOM: Great idea!

(Puppets exit stage)

* * *

"Inside Out" # 9.

SUMMARY: Mikie, who acts conceited because he can afford lots of nice clothes, doesn't want to play with kids who don't have nice clothes. His friend, Jenna, helps him see he may look good on the outside, but needs changes on the inside. (Based on 1 Samuel 16:7)

CHARACTERS: *(two puppets about seven to ten years old)*

    JENNA.....*a girl puppet friend*

    MIKIE...... *a boy puppet dressed in sharp clothes*

SETTING: *Outside the house one boy puppet appears dressed in very stylish clothes.*

JENNA: Hi, Mikie...you're looking real sharp. Are you going someplace important?

MIKIE: *(perturbed)* What do you mean? I always look like this.

JENNA: You don't dress like that to play around your house!

MIKE: Sure I do.

JENNA: Come on, you don't mow the lawn in good clothes.

MIKIE: *(getting more emphatic)* Sure, I do!

JENNA: Well, I know you don't play soccer in those clothes.

The Right Connection by Iris Gray Dowling

MIKIE: (*disgusted tone*) Sure... Why not?

JENNA: Cause you wear a soccer uniform.

MIKIE: I guess you got me there.

JENNA: My Mom makes me wear play clothes. She said I might get my clothes spoiled or torn, then I wouldn't be able to wear them to school.

MIKIE: No big deal! I'll throw those rags in the trash and buy new ones. I don't play with kids who don't dress nice.

JENNA: Don't you think that's wasteful and unkind? Some kids might not have parents who can afford so many new clothes.

MIKIE: That's not true these days. Everybody's got plenty of money.

JENNA: Wait a minute! You can't see past your new shirt. Lots of dads had to give up their good jobs to go fight a war. A girl in my class lost her father in the 9-11 terrorist disaster. Her mom doesn't have a job; and she has to take care of her little children.

MIKIE: Well, you made your point. I guess they didn't know that would happen. Wonder what we could do for them?

JENNA: Wow! Now your brain is perking.

MIKIE: (*He moves his head and body up and down like perking*) I'm perking in the right way, wouldn't you say?

JENNA: I hope we won't ever have their problems.

MIKIE: Yes, I agree we should do something to help those kids who lost their dads.

JENNA: I thought I'd send them some money, but we should think about people who have problems in our own neighborhood, too.

MIKIE: I don't know anybody like that.

JENNA: I'm glad my dad's able to work. There's a girl named Sarah in my Kid's Club. Her dad is real sick.

MIKIE: Can't her mom work?

JENNA: She has to take care of Sarah's dad. The medical treatment and operations cost so much that the insurance companies stopped paying for his medicines.

MIKIE: *(sighing)* Huh… I wasn't thinking about all that, just the kids I didn't want to be seen with.

JENNA: You mean the ones who wear the same clothes over and over?

MIKIE: Yeah, I thought they'd wear them until they fell off.

JENNA: Does it matter as long as they keep their clothes clean?

MIKIE: I want <u>my</u> friends to look sharp like me.

The Right Connection by Iris Gray Dowling

JENNA: Clothes are just a cover for our bodies, but the real person is deep inside where no one sees.

MIKIE: This is the real ME…just what you see!

JENNA: No, I'm not talking about flesh, bones, and clothes, but the unseen person that lives inside.

MIKIE: If I want to see inside, I'll get an MRI.

JENNA: MRI's won't show the inner person I'm talking about. I mean your attitude and the way you act toward others. That shows up way past your beautiful clothes.

MIKIE: The way I <u>look</u> makes an impression on my friends.

JENNA: The way you act does, too. Other people may see what you look like at first, but how you act soon makes them forget about your nice clothes.

MIKIE: I don't say much to those kids who don't dress nice.

JENNA: You don't have to. Your words and attitudes have already affected them. God calls that sin and sees us like filthy rags.

MIKIE: I never thought I had a bad attitude.

JENNA: In my Sunday school I learned how Jesus loved all kinds of people: rich and poor—sinners of the lowest kind; blind and sick; even maniacs and lepers who other people didn't want to get near.

MIKIE: That's what Jesus did—heal people. He was perfect; I can't be like him. I'll have to do things my way.

JENNA: He wants us to try to be more like him. Jesus not only healed sick bodies but sickness of the heart and mind.

MIKIE: What kind of sickness are you talking about?

JENNA: Sickness of mind--those who think they're better than others, *(pause)* those who need to learn more about Jesus' love and humble ways.

MIKIE: I guess I kinda thought like I was better than the other kids because I had better clothes.

JENNA: Your actions did speak pretty loud.

MIKIE: I didn't hear anything. *(pause)* But I get what you're saying.

JENNA: Did you know God saw you inside and He saw you wearing rags?

MIKIE: But I'm not acting like that anymore.

JENNA: Good actions speak louder than words, but God is the only one who can see deep inside us. He knows what we really think and feel before others see it in our actions.

MIKIE: That's a little scary. *(pause)* God saw that I needed a change before I knew it. *(pause)* I didn't realize I acted so bad. *(pause)* I'll ask God's forgiveness.

The Right Connection by Iris Gray Dowling

JENNA: Good, we all need to make changes sometimes. That's what God wants—change.

MIKIE: One more thing I'm going to do is give more than a dollar for the poor kids who lost their dads in terrorist attacks or war. I know I can do more than I've been doing.

JENNA: Now your brains are perking again. I'm with you! Let's get started on a project to help others.

(**BOTH** exit)

* * *

Follow-up Suggestions: Do you ever turn away from people whose clothes aren't as nice as yours? Maybe some of us need to think about our heart, and the words that come out of our mouths, or the way we act, or the places we go. God says it is what's in our heart that counts. A kind considerate attitude is more important than the latest fashion. Will you be a friend to that lonely, shy kid or the one who has a family problem? How do you treat the kids who don't have clothes as nice as yours?

Some helpful scriptures to use: Luke 18:9-14; 16:15; John 7:24; 1 Peter 3:3, 4. 1 Samuel 16:1-12 could be used for a suggested Bible lesson.

Suggested songs to sing with the puppets: "Oh Be Careful Little Mind", "What You Think", *CEF, Salvation Songs*.

"On The Rescue Team"   # 10.

SUMMARY: Mikie thinks he can be a rescue worker without training. Ami tells him how he can be a rescuer of sin sick people. (Based on John 3:16)

CHARACTERS: (*two puppets aged 7 to 10, or puppet and ventriloquist=vent*)

      AMI......*older puppet or vent*

      MIKIE...*younger puppet*

PROPS: *badge, rescuer's shirt (blue or gray)*

(**AMI** *enters first—If she plays the part of a vent, she first stands outside the puppet stage. If she plays the part of a puppet, she is inside the puppet stage.*)

AMI: I'm expecting a visitor today. He's a little shy. Let me go to the door and see if he's here yet. (***AMI*** *goes back stage to check on **MIKIE**.*)

MIKIE: (*hear voice from back stage*) I thought you'd never come to open the door.

AMI: (*says back stage*) We've been waiting for you. We didn't know you were outside the door waiting for us.

MIKIE: (*both enter*) Waiting is what I do a lot of.

The Right Connection by Iris Gray Dowling

AMI: What do you mean, Mikie?

MIKIE: I wait for the 911 calls. Then I help the rescue team save people's lives.

AMI: I wondered why you were dressed in that outfit.

MIKIE: You like it? (*pause; holds badge*) See my badge.

AMI: Did you take a course to learn rescue work?

MIKIE: No, I just got this badge from a friend.

AMI: Mikie, you can't wear that badge without some training in rescue work!

MIKIE: Why? When people are in trouble, they need to be rescued. They don't take time to find out if I had any training.

AMI: I guess, you're right about that. But you can't wear a badge telling you had training if you didn't.

MIKIE: Why not? I like this badge. (*clings to the badge*)

AMI: It's not honest. You might need to perform some life saving technique, like CPR, and you'd be expected to know how to do it.

MIKIE: (*shyly*) I didn't think about that. I was just pretending, like Ryan does when he pretends to be a fireman. (*Use a lively student's name.*)

AMI: All those jobs take special training. You learn the best way to save people's lives.

MIKIE: Oh...well...so much for that! They won't let me go to school. I'm just a dummy.

AMI: Don't say things like that, Mikie. I know something you can do to save lives and you don't need much training. Anyone can do it.

MIKIE: (*leans toward her*) Tell me about it.

AMI: It's bringing people to Jesus from a path of sin.

MIKIE: How do you know I can do that?

AMI: Anyone who has Jesus living in their heart has a badge to do that.

MIKIE: A badge?

AMI: Salvation's badge.

MIKIE: Oh-h-h...what a big word. It won't fit on a badge.

AMI: No, it's not on the badge. You wear it in your life. People see how you live, even if they can't see a badge.

MIKIE: Oh! That's different.

AMI: Salvation means Jesus saves us from sin. He is the master rescuer. He's willing to save anyone who will trust him.

The Right Connection by Iris Gray Dowling

MIKIE: Master rescuer?

AMI: Yes...He saves sinners from going to a place of punishment.

MIKIE: I don't understand what I can do then.

AMI: You tell them Jesus died for their sins and wants to save them so they can go to heaven with him someday.

MIKIE: Oh...that's all?

AMI: Tell them Jesus will forgive them of all their sins if they ask him.

MIKIE: Yeah?

AMI: That's all. They make a choice if they want to be rescued from sin or not. You can't save them, Jesus saves them. All you do is tell them.

MIKIE: I have to say that's a different kind of rescuing than I had in mind.

AMI: Even as the rescuer you were talking about, there are some people you can't help. Rescuers might try very hard, but in a bad flood, the strong current may sweep someone away from them.

MIKIE: Yeah, I know it happened to some people not long ago.

AMI: People all around us need Jesus to save them, but they might say, "Go away, you dummy, I don't want to hear that religion stuff." They choose to be swept away to eternity without God.

MIKIE: Hmm...That's different! I thought everybody in trouble wanted help, but I guess it's not true.

AMI: Sad, isn't it? God loves everyone and wants to rescue them from the dangers and punishment of sin...but they keep saying 'No' to God!

MIKIE: I can't believe there are people who refuse God's help.

AMI: Some think sinful things are fun. They don't want to give them up right away. Some think they are too young and have plenty of time.

MIKIE: But we don't know how long our life on earth will be, do we?

AMI: No, the Bible says, "Life is like a flower. It stays beautiful a little while, then it fades, and is gone."

MIKIE: I once saw a flood victim catching on to whatever he could, but he couldn't save himself.

AMI: Lots of people think they can save themselves and get to heaven their own way.

MIKIE: They do that?

AMI: Yeah...they try to live a good life, go to church and give lots of money to the poor...but none of this can save them...only Jesus can because he died for our sins on the cross.

The Right Connection by Iris Gray Dowling

MIKIE: I'm glad you told me about this kind of rescuing. I don't have to wait for the 911 calls anymore.

AMI: You're right, Mikie. People áll around us will never hear if we don't tell them.

MIKIE: How about you boys and girls? If you've said 'yes' to Jesus, you need to tell your friends how he can forgive and save them.

AMI: Mikie, didn't you plan to sing for us today?

MIKIE: Oh, I got so excited about my rescuing job, I forgot. Let's see, what was I going to sing? (*pause*) Oh-h-h...I know. (*sings*) * "Throw out the lifeline, Throw out the life line. There's someone you may rescue, some one you can save."

(***MIKIE*** *holds some musical notes too long.*)

AMI: That sounds a little mixed up. Let's look at this song book to see how it goes.

MIKIE: Okay. (*Sings: "Throw Out The Life-line", stanza 1 and 'refrain. Add a few holding notes.*) Now I've got to get to my rescuing. Time is short you know.

AMI: All right, Mikie. These kids understand. Come back again when you can.

MIKIE: Bye, boys and girls. (*exits*)

(*Ventriloquist or* ***Teacher*** *step beside the puppet stage.*)

* * *

(Follow-up done by Teacher or Vent):
Have you let Jesus rescue you from your sin? Or are you trying to save yourself by going to church every Sunday, giving your money to missionaries, or being a good kid? Those things can never save you. Jesus alone can save you if you ask him. *(pause)* Don't refuse him. Is there anyone who wants to ask Jesus to save them today?

* Suggested Song: "Throw Out The Life-line", E. S.Ufford, *Living Hymns.* Encore Pub. page 190.

11. "Who Is Your Hero?"

THEME: Looking for heroes.

SUMMARY: Mikie imitates his sports hero in the way he dresses and acts, but learns he should imitate someone much more important.

CHARACTERS: *(a girl and boy puppet aged seven to ten)*

    MIKIE…..*younger boy puppet, age 8*

    KATIE…..*puppet aged ten, neighbor*

PROPS: *Baseball; pen; baseball uniform (choose props for any sport)*

MIKIE: Good morning, Katie. (*skipping; cheery voice; carrying ball*)

KATIE: *(drooping mouth)* I don't see anything good about it.

MIKIE: I got a World Series baseball at last night's game.

KATIE: What's so great about that? And why are you wearing that silly looking outfit?

MIKIE: It's not silly! I wanna look like Erin. He's my favorite player.

The Right Connection by Iris Gray Dowling

KATIE: It's okay to like him, but is he somebody you want to act like or dress like?

MIKIE: Sure! Why not?

KATIE: Because you look silly.

MIKIE: I do not! I'm gonna be a great baseball player, just like him.

KATIE: Well, you're not there yet.

MIKIE: Just give me time. I'll make it.

KATIE: For your sake I hope so. It would be a shame to waste all that money for such fancy duds and then never wear them much.

MIKIE: Well, I'm wearing them now!

KATIE: Yeah, but I mean in a real game.

MIKIE: I play in a real game.

KATIE: I don't mean Little League, I mean in a big league.

MIKIE: I'm goin to one of them next week.

KATIE: But not to play, Silly!

MIKIE: No, but I'm gonna wear my baseball uniform, so I can pretend I'm Erin.

KATIE: Don't you think it would be better if you thought a little more about the person you want to be like?

MIKIE: I did think about Erin. He's a good player.

KATIE: You could have picked someone who didn't get arrested.

MIKIE: When did Erin get arrested?

KATIE: It was all over the news a few weeks ago.

MIKIE: I didn't hear anything about it.

KATIE: Well you did now. You were so busy looking and acting like him, you didn't hear anything else.

MIKIE: Okay. Now you're happy that you messed up my dreams.

KATIE: No, I just wanted to give you something to think about. Who else would you want to look like or act like?

MIKIE: Do you have a better idea?

KATIE: Pick someone you would be proud to imitate.

MIKIE: None of the sports stars are perfect.

KATIE: No-o-o.

MIKIE: The TV and movie stars certainly aren't either.

KATIE: I guess you haven't had your eyes shut all the time, have you?

MIKIE: No. I don't think I can find any group that has a perfect person.

KATIE: Well. I guess you're right, but Jesus was. If you try to act like Him, you can't go wrong.

MIKIE: Jesus wasn't a sports player. Say, didn't He get arrested, too?

KATIE: Yeah, but that's different. The religious leaders of that day tried to trick Him into doing or saying something wrong so they could find fault with Him. Even the ruler, Pilate, and his wife could see that He was innocent of any wrong.

MIKIE: Why did they arrest Him then?

KATIE: The religious leaders kept accusing Him. They got one of the disciples to betray Him. Finally, they arrested Him, put Him on trial, and crucified Him, when He wasn't guilty of any wrong.

MIKIE: How could they do that to someone that wasn't guilty?

KATIE: Self-righteous men wanted to be popular, not honest, I guess.

MIKIE: Why didn't Jesus defend himself?

KATIE: He knew He had to fulfill God's plan, that He had to die on the cross for our sins. If He hadn't, we couldn't be saved.

MIKIE: Saved?

KATIE: Yeah, saved from the penalty of our sins.

MIKIE: How could his dying on the cross save me from my sins?

KATIE: Jesus died in your place. The Bible says "The wages of sin is death". You see, Jesus died so you wouldn't have to die to pay for your own sins.

MIKIE: He had to care a lot for me, to do that.

KATIE: Only a real friend would care that much.

MIKIE: Wow! There aren't many friends who would die for someone else. That is the kind of person I should imitate as my hero.

KATIE: You've got the right idea now. Those who follow Jesus should try to dress and act like he would want them to.

MIKIE: Is there an outfit that I should wear as a follower of Jesus?

KATIE: No, but the Bible tells us modesty is important--not to wear revealing clothes like a lot of the popular singers and TV characters.

MIKIE: I don't think I see Christians who look much different from any one else these days.

KATIE: We should see a difference and set an example of modesty, though. We should be careful not to draw attention away from the Lord by displaying tattoos and jewelry.

MIKIE: What's wrong with them?

KATIE: Will they make people think about Jesus? He wants us to be his salt and light on this earth.

MIKIE: So the way I act and dress can tell a lot about what I believe?

KATIE: Yes, Christians are supposed to show the love of Jesus, not love of themselves.

MIKIE: Oh, I see what you mean. If I show myself, I'm not letting people see Jesus is living in me.

KATIE: Finally you got it. It's like a song I learned in Kid's Club. "A Sermon in Shoes". What I do and how I dress tells others what I really believe. It's like I'm preaching a sermon wherever I walk.

MIKIE: That's an interesting way of putting it. I think I heard that song once. It goes "You're a sermon in shoes………."

KATIE: Let's try singing it together.

MIKIE: I think I can still wear my sports clothes. I just have to remember who my leader is.

KATIE: You got it. That baseball uniform is okay, if your looks and actions please Jesus.

MIKIE: Got ya. Now I'd like you to sign my baseball so I can remember you helped me see Jesus is the one I should imitate.

The Right Connection by Iris Gray Dowling

KATIE: Thanks, Mikie. I'd be honored. (*takes pen to sign the ball*)

(**BOTH** *exit*)

* * *

Suggested Bible verses: Romans 6:23; 1 Peter 3:3-5; Matthew 5:13-16.

Suggested Song: "You're a Sermon in Shoes", *Salvation Songs* #4, page 56

"Lasting Forever"   # 12.

THEME: Extinct or eternity?

SUMMARY: Mikie wants to get people to save the earth and its resources, but he learns it's important for people to know about God's plans

CHARACTERS: (*two puppets between 7 and ten years old*)

    MIKIE….. *a boy puppet*

    SARAH…. *a girl playmate puppet*

(*MIKIE wears a T-shirt with earth environment theme on it. He has fliers in his hand*)

SARAH: *(enters)* Hi, Mikie. That's an odd outfit you're wearing.

MIKIE: What do you mean odd? I'm going to save our earth.

SARAH: What? Why save the earth? Don't you know God created the earth and cares for it?

MIKIE: Sure I know that, but since people don't take care of it, some plants and animals have become extinct.

SARAH: Well, I don't like stinky animals anyway.

MIKIE: Not stinky animals!

The Right Connection by Iris Gray Dowling

SARAH: Oh you mean stinky plants like skunk cabbage.

MIKIE: No, No, No! That's not what extinct means.

SARAH: Yeah, I know like dinosaurs aren't around anymore.

MIKIE: I don't mean them either. That was ages ago. I mean animals and birds we have today. Lots of them are in danger of disappearing forever. We need to do something before it's too late.

SARAH: I'll bet you can't name one animal or plant that's ready to disappear.

MIKIE: Sure can too! It's in the news all the time. I heard last week that the macaw is extinct. They can't find any more in the jungles of South America. Remember the eagles, our national bird. They're protected so they won't become extinct.

SARAH: Yeah, we heard a lot about eagles. Can you name a plant that's in danger?

MIKIE: My Mom told me about a little white flower called an arbutus. Mom used to find them along the road banks near wooded areas when she walked home from school. They used to be real plentiful until people cut down too many trees to build roads and houses. Now we can't find arbutus flowers.

SARAH: Did you ever see one?

MIKIE: My Mom and Dad tried to show me one on our last camping trip. But they couldn't find a single one.

SARAH: That doesn't prove it's extinct.

MIKIE: Maybe not, but it happens to lots of animals and plants before people realize they disappeared . People think it's more important to build houses and roads even if they destroy the natural homes of animals and plants.

SARAH: Oh, I hadn't thought of that.

MIKIE: Well, I did. So I'm going to put up these posters. I want people to learn how to take care of our earth and its resources.

SARAH: Posters can do that?

MIKIE: These posters tell about meetings at the library. Then I'll ask the librarian to put out articles and books about nature becoming extinct. We'll get a speaker to help people learn to save our earth.

SARAH: That all sounds good, but how about those very people who might be in danger.

MIKIE: What people do you mean?

SARAH: You didn't think about all those people's souls that are in danger.

MIKIE: What are you talking about?

SARAH: If they reject Jesus they will face eternal death and punishment.

MIKIE: No one wants that.

The Right Connection by Iris Gray Dowling

SARAH: God wants us to take care of the earth he made, but the Bible says the earth won't last forever. God said he will make a new earth for those who follow him.

MIKIE: A new earth?

SARAH: But everyone won't get to live on the new earth.

MIKIE: Really? Who will?

SARAH: Only the ones who believe in Jesus while they're here on this earth.

MIKIE: Doesn't everybody believe in Jesus?

SARAH: They might believe he lived, but don't really believe he can save them from their sins, so they don't accept him.

MIKIE: I get ya. They need to be saved by God's salvation plan.

SARAH: Right! Some people will never get saved if they don't chose to ask God's forgiveness for their sins. Their separation from God will almost be like being extinct.

MIKIE: Hmm…That's something to think about all right. If I worked to save all the animals and plants on earth, but forgot about all those people who will miss heaven, then my work won't be worth much after all.

SARAH: It's good to take care of the earth God gave us, but since the earth won't last forever, it's better to do what will last for all eternity.

MIKIE: Oh, I'm sure glad I met you to help me see how important it is to think about people getting ready to meet the Lord.

SARAH: Think about Bill, your best friend. Where will he be for all eternity?

MIKIE: I want him to live forever in heaven with me. I don't want him to disappear forever like those extinct plants and animals or be in darkness forever.

SARAH: There are many more people you and I know who aren't on their way to heaven.

MIKIE: I'm going to do something about that. I can't tell everybody, but I'll ask the Lord to help me tell more people than I have in the past. I can change these fliers to ones that tell about spending eternity with God.

SARAH: I'm sure God will be pleased that you decided to care about how people will spend eternity.

MIKIE: I better go and get to work on my new papers. See you later. *(exits)*

* * *

ANNOUNCER: How about you boys and girls? Do you have any friends you think aren't going to heaven? Did you think they may not know very much about who Jesus really is, or that He will forgive their sins? Who is going to tell them? Maybe the Lord wants <u>*you*</u> to tell them. Let's pray and ask the Lord to help us.

The Right Connection by Iris Gray Dowling

#13.   "READY FOR HEAVEN"

THEME: Heaven

SUMMARY: Mikie, a shy boy, is afraid to have the kids look at him, but with the help of his sister, Amy, they talk about heaven and the importance of being ready to go there. *(Based on Revelation 20:15; 21:27; John 14:1-6)*

CHARACTERS: *(two puppets or a ventriloquist (vent) and humanoid puppet.)*

   AMY..... *girl puppet about nine years old*

   MIKIE... *boy puppet one year younger, her brother*

AMY: (*enters; talks to kids before **MIKIE** comes*) We have a visitor today. I need to tell you he's a little shy. Do you think you could be real quiet so you won't scare him when he comes in? *(pause)* Hey, maybe if you close your eyes until he gets in the room, he'll feel better. Keep them closed until I tell you to open them.

MIKIE: (*shyly enters, stops, and whispers*) Look! *(pause)* <u>Brian's</u> eyes are open. (*Use name of bold student.*)

AMY: That's O.K. You aren't going to let him scare you, are you?

MIKIE: (*with shaky voice*) Seeing his eyes makes me shiver.

(**MIKIE** *pulls back.*)

The Right Connection by Iris Gray Dowling

AMY: All right, close your eyes, Brian. (or *other student's name; pause*) Come in, Mikie. (*pauses as he enters and stares at the kids*) Mikie, when can I tell the kids to open their eyes?

MIKIE: I don't know. That's your problem.

AMY: No, it's not. It's yours! I just want to know when you're going to let them see you?

MIKIE: It doesn't matter to me if they open their eyes.

AMY: Okay, Mikie. I'll tell them to open their eyes and say, hello.

MIKIE: *(shaky voice)* Waaait...Let me cover my eyes. I can't stand people looking at me.

AMY: Okay, You cover your eyes, so I can tell them to open theirs.

MIKIE: If they do, I'll run out of here.

AMY: No you won't! You're just kidding.

MIKIE: Oh, you think I'm kidding?

AMY: If you run away you'll show everybody what a coward you are.

MIKIE: Yeah. *(pause)* I–I--I think I'm getting a little braver.

AMY: It's about time!

MIKIE: You know… I bet they're scared to look at me.

The Right Connection by Iris Gray Dowling

AMY: No, they aren't. (*says toward the kids*) Okay, kids, open your eyes.

MIKIE: I saw that odd look on their faces when they opened their eyes. Do I look that bad? (*looks at the vent*)

AMY: No, Mikie. They just waited so long and finally they got to see you. Some of them probably didn't see you the last time you came.

MIKIE: When did I come before?

AMY: It was just a few weeks ago. Did you forget your memory cap?

MIKIE: (p*uts hand on head*) I don't think so!

AMY: Did you learn your verse for today?

MIKIE: Sure, I'm no dummy.

AMY: Why don't you say it, then?

MIKIE: What's the verse?

AMY: You said you knew it. (*straightens **MIKIE**'s hair*) What are you trying to pull?

MIKIE: You're the one pulling my hair. (*pause; shakes head; looks at **AMY***)

AMY: No, I'm just pushing it back off your forehead.

The Right Connection by Iris Gray Dowling

MIKIE: I really do know the verse.

AMY: Well, say it then.

MIKIE: Jesus said, "In my Father's house are many mansions...I go to prepare a place for you. And if I go and prepare a place for you, I will come and get you so you can be there with me. (*John 14:2*)

AMY: That's pretty good, Mikie. But you put your own ending, didn't you?

MIKIE: Well, that's what Jesus meant. Now, it's your turn.

AMY: I think it's a good idea if we talk a little more about heaven.

MIKIE: That's the place everybody goes when they die, right?

AMY: Not everybody. Only those who believe in Jesus as their Savior.

MIKIE: Oh! When my cat died, every body said he went to cat heaven.

AMY: Maybe, but not God's Heaven. A cat is an animal that doesn't have a soul and spirit like people do. God didn't create animals just like people.

MIKIE: A soul and spirit? What's that mean?

AMY: God made people with a physical earthly body and a soul and spirit inside. People can choose to accept Jesus or not. Animals can't make that choice.

MIKIE: (*looks questioningly at AMY*) OOOh!

AMY: When we die our soul and spirit go to heaven. Our earthly body waits in the grave for the new body God will give us.

MIKIE: A new body, huh? Why not keep the one I have now?

AMY: It's sinful, not fit to go to a perfect heaven. God's going to change us with a new sinless body to last forever.

MIKIE: Oh, that sounds exciting. What else can you tell me about heaven?

AMY: It's a place with gold streets and light all the time--no darkness...no sickness...no pain...no sadness...just a double, double awesome place to be.

MIKIE: When I get to heaven. Do you think I'll get scared anymore?

AMY: No, you won't have any more fear or crying.

MIKIE: With a place like that to look forward to, why wouldn't I want to go there?

AMY: There's a lot we don't know about heaven, but God did tell us he wants to make a special place for us, and he wants us to be ready to go there.

MIKIE: We're ready, aren't we?

AMY: We need to make sure our name is written in the Book of Life, which God has in heaven.

MIKIE: How can I write my name in a book that's up in heaven?

AMY: By asking Jesus to forgive your sins and accepting him as your Savior. Then God writes your name in his Book of Life.

MIKIE: I DID that! So my name IS written there!

AMY: That's right. Let's see if we can sing a song about that before we leave today. I'll start singing. ""Is my name written there, on the page white and fair?"

MIKIE: (*repeats after AMY. Starts singing with wrong melody and draws some words out longer than necessary to be funny.*) "Is my name written there, on the page white and fair-r-r-r-r? Up in heaven in God's book. That's where!"

AMY: Mikie! It's a beautiful song! Why did you mess it up like that?

MIKIE: Does it really matter how I sing it? I told the truth.

AMY: It does matter...if you want people to listen. (*pause to get book*) Let's try it again. (*starts song and sings through with MIKIE cutting in; can prerecord*).

MIKIE: (*finishes singing*) Up in heaven! That's where! (*pause*) Let's go now. Singing in front of people makes me shiver. (*starts pulling toward the door*)

AMY: Bye, boys and girls. Be sure your name is in God's Book of Life so we'll meet again in heaven someday.

The Right Connection by Iris Gray Dowling

(*Both wave and Exit*)

* * *

** Suggested refrain from : "Is My Name Written There?" *Child Evangelism Fellowship--Salvation Songs #3*, page 39 or 82.

"Born Blind" # 14.

THEME: Physical and spiritual blindness analogy

SUMMARY: Benjie tells about his friend born blind and the blind man in the Bible as compared to being born spiritually blind. (Based on John 9)

CHARACTERS: *(two puppets, aged 7-10, or a ventriloquist and humanoid puppet)*

    BENJIE...*older boy puppet, or ventriloquist (vent)*

    ALLIE.... *girl puppet a little younger*

BENJIE: *(enters with blindfold on)*

ALLIE: What are you trying to prove wearing those things?

BENJIE: I was finding out how it feels to be like my friend who has never seen me.

ALLIE: *(questioning)* He has never seen you?

BENJIE: No. He was born blind.

ALLIE: Oh…that's too bad!

BENJIE: Well, he doesn't think so.

The Right Connection by Iris Gray Dowling

ALLIE: Really? I wouldn't want to be blind.

BENJIE: I wouldn't either, but he went to Blind School. He learned to play the piano and type on the computer from a recording machine. I can't do that.

ALLIE: Neither can I.

BENJIE: He reads lots of books written in Braille and listens to audio classics. He's gotten a better education than I have.

ALLIE: Braille's hard. I tried to read some Braille once, but I couldn't feel the dots.

BENJIE: It's hard for sighted people, but blind people seem to have an extra sense of touch. They study hard at blind school and learn skills so they can have a job.

ALLIE: You say your friend wouldn't want to be able to see?

BENJIE: No, he has learned how to live and work without seeing and he would need to change all he knows.

ALLIE: Oh, that makes sense, I guess.

BENJIE: I'm playing a trick on the kids so they can't see me.

ALLIE: What?

BENJIE: They can't see me!

ALLIE: That's what I thought you said. What's wrong with you? They can see you!

BENJIE: No they can't.

ALLIE: Yes, they can!

BENJIE: No, they can't!!

ALLIE: You must be a little mixed up. You can't see them.

BENJIE: Oh, I guess you're right.

ALLIE: Being blind isn't funny. Why do you want to do that?

BENJIE: I have my reasons. Some kids need to be kind to other kids who have problems.

ALLIE: That's true. But it doesn't sound like your blind friend wants much sympathy, so do you have another reason?

BENJIE: I was just giving the kids an idea what it feels like not to see.

ALLIE: Oh Benjie, you're so smart. Why did you do that?

BENJIE: I wanted to tell them about the blind man in the Bible. He was born blind and they didn't have blind schools, so he became a beggar. That's what happened to blind people throughout most of history.

ALLIE: And beggars were outcasts, so he wasn't happy about that, was he?

BENJIE: No, but Jesus was.

ALLIE: Did you say that made Jesus happy? I thought Jesus loved people and helped them so they wouldn't suffer.

BENJIE: He did, but the Bible says God let this man be born blind so He could teach people some spiritual lessons.

ALLIE: There you go with double answers again. (*pause*) What lessons?

BENJIE: Some people are born to see, but really don't see.

ALLIE: There you go—mixed up again.

BENJIE: No, I'm not. They can't see Jesus is the Son of God. So they are blind and don't know it.

ALLIE: How could they not know it?

BENJIE: Their physical eyes can see, but their spiritual eyes are blind.

ALLIE: Oh, I get it. They need to see through God's eyes that they are sinners and need His forgiveness.

BENJIE: Remember? (*sings*) "Amazing Grace, how sweet the sound, That saved a wretch like me. I once was lost, but now I'm found; Was blind, but now I see". *[1]

ALLIE: Now I get what that song means.

BENJIE: Good. That's why the man was born blind. God said in John 9:3 that He wanted to get glory for Himself. In other words He wanted people to see that God could open blind eyes. You see, those people were spiritually blind and the beggars were physically blind.

ALLIE: They didn't want to stay blind, did they?

BENJIE: Not the beggars.

ALLIE: I see. No one wanted to stay physically blind, but it's harder to help spiritually blind people.

BENJIE: Now you're perking. Spiritually blind people don't realize they're blind, so that's why they don't want help.

ALLIE: Then there are other people who are sinners and want to ask Jesus to forgive their sins.

BENJIE: They are no longer blind.

ALLIE: It's interesting that some people don't want to have sight, just like your friend. They are content to live in their spiritual blindness.

BENJIE: We need to pray for God to open their spiritual eyes and help them see.

ALLIE: Then God will open their eyes so they can see?

BENJIE: If they are willing, God will make them see. Just like the two blind men who followed Jesus. They begged Him to help them see. (*Luke 18: 38, 39*)

ALLIE: Now I SEE. If I have faith to believe and ask God to help me see the truth in His Word, I will SEE it.

BENJIE: You got it! Allie, you're so smart! We really need to help people see this truth or they will never realize they need more than physical sight.

ALLIE: Go ahead and use your blindfold. Maybe somebody will get the point. Jesus used all kinds of ways to help people see spiritual truths.

BENJIE: You're right. If you help one person see spiritually, God will be happy. (*puts blindfold on and reaches out with both hands to walk forward*) Where is the door? Where are those boys and girls we are supposed to talk to?

ALLIE: Right here, Benjie, (*takes his hand to guide him*)

BENJIE: Are they looking at me? (*pause*) I don't like people staring at me. (*pause*)

ALLIE: Benjie wants you all to cover your eyes and see if you like living in darkness.

BENJIE: Is it fun to live in the dark, boys and girls?

BOYS & GIRLS: No.

BENJIE: Let's take our blindfolds off and see what God says in His Bible. We'll look in John 9:35-37? (*find and read the verses*) Do all of you believe that Jesus is God's Son?

BOYS & GIRLS: Yes.

BENJIE: That's good. We can all see physically and spiritually. Just because we were born spiritually blind doesn't mean we have to stay that way.

ALLIE: You're right! God provided salvation and light through His Son, Jesus. If we believe, we are no longer blind. (*See John 9:5*)

BENJIE: I've worked so hard trying to act blind, my eyes are trying to close. I hope I'm not going blind.

ALLIE: Oh, no, you just need to get more sleep. Why don't you go take a nap now?

BENJIE: Okay. Bye, boys and girls. I'll come back when I get rested. *(he exits)*

ALLIE: Now I need to go too. (ALLIE *exits*)

* * *

*1 "Amazing Grace," John Newton, *Living Hymns*, Encore Publications Inc. page 187.

Scripture suggestions: John 9; Luke 18:38, 39.

The Right Connection by Iris Gray Dowling

#15. "A Robber Asks Forgiveness"

THEME: Forgiveness

SUMMARY: A conversation on the forgiveness of Onesimus makes our puppets see they need to forgive and forgive again. (Based on Philemon 8-21; Colossians 4:7-9)

COSTUMES: Puppets dress like Biblical characters in Colossae in 62 AD.

CHARACTERS: (*two puppets act as children in Philemon's household*)

    BENJIE…..*a boy puppet 7 to 10 years old.*

    AUTIE…..*a puppet one year older*

AUTIE: Did your hear Onesimus came home?

BENJIE: What? (*emphatic*) I thought he'd never come back after stealing from our master, Philemon.

AUTIE: The rumor is that Philemon accepted him with open arms. (*opens arms wide*)

BENJIE: After being robbed by him?

AUTIE: You know Philemon is a Christian and has a forgiving heart.

BENJIE: Does that mean he'll forgive the rest of the servants if we do something wrong like that?

AUTIE: He's not a foolish man. So we servants shouldn't be foolish either.

BENJIE: Well, how did Onesimus get in his good favor?

AUTIE: I heard he ran away after he stole from Philemon. He headed for Rome, over a thousand miles away.

BENJIE: I guess he thought that was far enough away not to get caught.

AUTIE: He didn't count on meeting the missionary, Paul, a good friend of Philemon's.

BENJIE: So Paul caught him?

AUTIE: No, God caught him. Onesimus heard Paul speak about servants honoring their masters and that stealing was sin. Paul said a sinner needs God's forgiveness.

BENJIE: Oh, he felt guilty. *(pause)* How did Paul know Onesimus was listening?

AUTIE: He didn't. God spoke through Paul to convict Onesimus' heart. Then Onesimus told Paul what he had done. He first asked if he could be Paul's servant.

BENJIE: Did he think Paul would accept him after admitting he was a robber?

The Right Connection by Iris Gray Dowling

AUTIE: Actually, Paul did forgive him because Onesimus asked God's forgiveness.

BENJIE: Wow! What a coincidence that he met Paul!

AUTIE: Not in God's eyes—Paul was in Rome living under house arrest waiting to appear before Caesar.

BENJIE: House arrest? That means he couldn't go away from the house.

AUTIE: No, but he was allowed to teach the people who came to listen.

BENJIE: I wonder how Onesimus found him there?

AUTIE: God made that happen eventhough they both were thousands of miles from home.

BENJIE: So Paul let Onesimus stay in his house to work?

AUTIE: Only long enough to wait for Paul to write a letter for him to carry to his master, Philemon. Paul told Onesimus he needed to make his sin right with God and with the one he had wronged.

BENJIE: Wow! Now does he want to stay?

AUTIE: He knows he needs to do what God wants him to do.

BENJIE: So God made a change in his life and in his thinking. (*pause; puts finger up to his head*) Have you heard how Philemon felt when he saw him?

AUTIE: Paul sent a letter and asked Philemon to forgive him. Paul said he'd pay the debt when he came back to Colossae.

BENJIE: Oh! Philemon forgave Onesimus because Paul asked him to?

AUTIE: No, he did it because God wanted him too. *(pause)* As Christians we all need to forgive others. Paul set that example for us.

BENGIE: So did Philemon.

AUTIE: Yes, you're right. Jesus said we should forgive seventy times seven.

BENJIE: I guess that means a lot of forgiving. *(pause)* Now I need to go.

AUTIE: Why so fast?

BENJIE: I have someone I need to forgive.

AUTIE: Oh…*(pause)* You better go then.

BENJIE: *(exits)* Bye, boys and girls. I'll come back when I make my wrong right.

AUTIE: Maybe I need to think about my own actions. Good-bye, now. *(exits)*

* * *

The Right Connection by Iris Gray Dowling

16. "The Surprise Sports Star"

THEME: Trusting God. *(Can be used for Grandparent's Day.)*

SUMMARY: Dad arranged to have a surprise visitor. The kids expected a sports star, not their grandpa, but enjoyed the Bible story about David's young life. (Based on I Samuel 16, 17)

CHARACTERS: *(two child puppets and one older puppet)*

>**JONNY**.....*puppet, age 9*

>**EMILY**..... *girl puppet, age 8*

>**GRANDPA**.... *older grandparent puppet*

*AT RISE: **Jonny** and **Emily** talk about Dad's surprise.*

JONNY: Dad said he invited a mystery guest for dinner.

EMILY: I wonder who it is.

JONNY: It's too bad Mom is sick and can't come to eat dinner with us.

EMILY: I think it's that hockey player that visited the middle school today.

JONNY: What makes you think that?

EMILY: Dad works at the school, doesn't he?

JONNY: We'll soon find out. I guess Mom wouldn't care about missing dinner with a sports person.

EMILY: Let's pretend we're surprised when he comes.

JONNY: Okay. I can't believe Dad kept this secret.

EMILY: *(a knock is heard;* **Emily** *jumps up)* Sh-sh-sh. The guest is here!

JONNY: *(whispers)* Where's Dad?

EMILY: He's in the kitchen fixing dinner.

JONNY: Sh-sh-sh! Let's be quiet. We don't want to scare the guest.

EMILY: You said it. *(They hear a loud knock again; runs to open the door; her mouth flies open)* Look, who's here, Jonny.

JONNY: Why-y-y… It's Grandpa. *(stutters)* C-c-come in.

GRANDPA: You look surprised.

JONNY: We didn't know you were coming tonight.

GRANDPA: I thought your father needed me.

JONNY: Oh! Dad's in the kitchen.

EMILY: I really don't think Dad needs any help, though. He told us he invited a surprise visitor.

The Right Connection by Iris Gray Dowling

GRANDPA: So, I surprised you, didn't I?

EMILY: You sure did! But I meant another visitor.

JONNY: You're not the surprise person are you?

GRANDPA: You weren't expecting me, were you?

JONNY: No, but…

GRANDPA: That's why I'm a surprise visitor. How come I get the feeling you are disappointed?

JONNY: Oh, no. We thought it was the sports star who was at Dad's school today.

GRANDPA: I'm not a sports star now, but I played lots of sports when I was young. I hope I'm another kind of star now. (***GRANDPA*** *hugs the two kids*)

EMILY: You are, Grandpa.

GRANDPA: That's what I want to hear. I want to be your star.

JONNY: Come over here, Grandpa. You can sit in Dad's big chair.

GRANDPA: Thanks, Jonny. *(pause)* Why don't you both sit beside me?

JONNY: *(**CHILDREN** sit close to **GRANDPA**)* I heard you liked to read the Bible, Grandpa.

GRANDPA: Oh, yes. When I was a kid there weren't many books. At school I read every book I could get, but at home I had to work on the farm.

EMILY: We like to hear about those days, Grandpa.

GRANDPA: There weren't many libraries close by and we couldn't get to them as easily as you can today. We had one book at my house that I didn't have to get at the library.

JONNY: I know what that book was—the Bible!

GRANDPA: That's right, my boy. It sounds like you've heard about my childhood before.

JONNY: I did hear that part, but I like to hear it again.

EMILY: *(gets Bible from small table)* Here, Grandpa.

EMILY: Can you read this to us since Dad is busy?.

GRANDPA: I'd be glad to. Everything I heard from the Bible certainly influenced my life. I pray it will do the same for my children and grandchildren.

JONNY: Did your father read to you, Grandpa?

GRANDPA: Actually he did. Sometimes I can still hear his voice reading to me.

JONNY: Will you tell us one of the stories you liked best?

The Right Connection by Iris Gray Dowling

GRANDPA: I'd be glad to. (***CHILDREN'S** eyes on **GRANDPA***) Since you were expecting a sports star, why don't I read about one of those?

JONNY: I didn't know the Bible had any sports stars.

GRANDPA: Oh, yes. There were many who had strong bodies. One was David He spent his young life in the fields caring for his father's sheep.

EMILY: I thought he just sat on a rock while the sheep ate grass.

GRANDPA: Yes, he did that sometimes, but he had to keep track of every sheep and climb the high rocks and look for them if any got lost. The kids of today do rock climbing in a gym room, but David did it for real.

JONNY: I thought he played a harp.

GRANDPA: Oh yes, he played the harp very well. He wrote many songs praising God.

JONNY: How do you know that?

GRANDPA: His songs are recorded in the Psalms and other books of the Bible. He used his spare time to practice the harp and become good, even good enough to play for the King. God gave him talent, but he had to develop it.

JONNY: Oh! How old was David during this story?

GRANDPA: A teenager. He knew who God was and spent a lot of time talking to God and meditating on the scriptures he remembered from hearing his family read them.

JONNY: It seems like David kept busy out there in the fields.

GRANDPA: There were times he had to rescue his sheep from the mouth of a bear or lion. He killed those big animals to save his precious sheep. That shows he cared about his job and didn't want to lose one single sheep.

EMILY: I guess that's why his father gave him that job.

GRANDPA: Not exactly. He was the youngest of eight sons of Jesse. All those older brothers thought he was a little kid and a weakling.

JONNY: But God put him out in the fields and gave him lots of experiences to show he wasn't a weakling, right?

GRANDPA: He learned responsibility and learned to trust God every day. There is so much I like about David. He learned to be humble and enjoy being where God put him.

JONNY: What else shows David was an athlete.

GRANDPA: Well, everyone knows about Goliath, the giant. David didn't kill that nine-foot man alone, but by trusting God. God helped him use his skills to gain a great victory.

JONNY: Is there anything else you like about David?

The Right Connection by Iris Gray Dowling

GRANDPA: Yes. God wasn't pleased with King Saul and told the prophet Samuel to anoint a new king from among Jesse's sons.

EMILY: So there were eight men to choose from. How would Samuel know which one?

GRANDPA: He didn't know, but knew God would show him. Jesse brought his seven older sons and marched them in front of Samuel, but God didn't tell Samuel to anoint any of them.

EMILY: Samuel must have felt a little foolish with all those big strong men standing in front of him. (*giggles*)

GRANDPA: This is the great part of the story. Samuel asked if there was another son. Jesse said there was a younger son out in the field with the sheep. He was probably thinking, "Surely you don't want him." Then Samuel commanded them to bring him. When he saw David he said, "This is the one God wants me to anoint".

EMILY: All those other guys must have been disappointed.

JONNY: But God was getting David ready for a big job, wasn't He?

GRANDPA: Yes, that's what is so good about this story. God knew what was in David's heart and He brought him out of the practice field when He was ready to use him somewhere else. David went through a lot more preparation before he actually sat on the throne.

JONNY: I guess I'll try not to complain when I have to practice music or sports. I need that preparation for God to use me when he is ready.

GRANDPA: It's good you see that God works in our lives, too. We don't just jump into a big successful job.

JONNY: Grandpa, you really are the best sports star.

GRANDPA: I learned as I read the Bible when I was a young man that it was important to trust God if I wanted Him to trust me.

JONNY: That's what I want, too.

GRANDPA: God wants all of us to be prepared to serve Him. As you can see with David, we don't have to wait until we're grown up. God used David a lot in his young years.

EMILY: I'm happy you came to be our surprise visitor tonight. I'm glad you showed me that I can be someone God can use even when I'm young.

JONNY: Will you come back and tell us more of these stories sometime?

GRANDPA: I'll be glad to. Next time it doesn't have to be a surprise plan! (*GRANDPA hugs the children and goes off SR-- Lights down*)

* * *

The Right Connection by Iris Gray Dowling

17. "A GOOD TIP"

SUMMARY: Ethan learns the importance of carrying God's Word in his heart. (*Based on Psalms 119:2, 9-11, 16, 105*)

CHARACTERS: (*two puppets, or a humanoid puppet and ventriloquist=vent*)

>**EMILY**....*girl puppet or girl vent*

>**ETHAN**...*boy puppet or humanoid puppet*

ETHAN: (*acts happy; carries favorite toy*) Good morning, boys and girls.

EMILY: I'm glad you're being so friendly this morning, Ethan.

ETHAN: Can't you see? I'm happy!

EMILY: Why are you so happy?

ETHAN: You let me bring my favorite toy.

EMILY: Did you understand what I said?

ETHAN: What do you mean?

EMILY: I said you could bring it, but if you leave it somewhere. I don't want to see tears.

ETHAN: I won't forget it. My brain is tip-top.

EMILY: You think it's better than the one God gave me?

ETHAN: Sure!

EMILY: I'll bet you can't say as many Bible verses as I can.

ETHAN: I'll bet I can!

EMILY: Okay, boys and girls, you keep score. (*pause*) Ready? Ethan, you go first.

ETHAN: Uh...uh...uh...uh...(*rolls eyes upward*)

EMILY: What's wrong, Ethan? Did you forget?

ETHAN: No. Uh...uh...uh... (*looks down with a frown.*)

EMILY: E-e-e-than, can't you think of one?

ETHAN: Uh-huh.

EMILY: Well, say it then.

ETHAN: Not right now.

EMILY: Well, I guess I won.

ETHAN: But you didn't say a verse either.

EMILY: Okay, I'll say one. Psalm 119:11, "I have hidden your word in my heart, that I might not sin against you."

ETHAN: (*claps*)

EMILY: Now, I won. Okay?

ETHAN: Not yet, I got one. "I will not neglect your Word".

EMILY: Good, Ethan. The verse also says, "I will delight in your statutes".

ETHAN: Statues? We don't worship statues.

EMILY: I know, Ethan. The word is not "statues", but "statutes". It's got three "t's" It means "God's Words"?

ETHAN: Oh! (*pause*) It says we should be happy to study God's words.

EMILY: Now you understand. (*pause*) I let you carry your favorite toy because it made you happy. Learning God's Word will make you happy, too.

ETHAN: I thought of something more important to carry with me—my Bible!

EMILY: Don't you see? Not just carry it in your hand, but in your heart and mind.

ETHAN: Okay...you made your point. I should carry my Bible to church, instead of a toy.

EMILY: I made two points.

ETHAN: What else?

EMILY: You should carry God's Word with you all the time by being able to say it.

ETHAN: Okay. I won't forget my Bible next Sunday, and I'll try to learn some verses.

EMILY: Good, Ethan. I'll try to learn more verses, too. I need God's words to help me at school, and on the school bus, or where ever I go. I need to remember what God wants me to do.

ETHAN: You sure need it a lot more than I do.

EMILY: Why do you say that? Just because I go to school doesn't mean I need it more.

ETHAN: Well, I don't do anything but sit here all by myself.

EMILY: That's when you have time to think wrong things, look at wrong magazines, or watch wrong pictures on TV.

ETHAN: You're right, I didn't think of that. (*to kids*) I'm going to learn more Bible verses so I can have them at the tip of my brain when I need them. (*points to his head*)

EMILY: Ethan, what a good tip to leave with these boys and girls.

ETHAN: You mean I have to go? Just when I'm getting good!

The Right Connection by Iris Gray Dowling

EMILY: Do you want to say another verse before you go?

ETHAN: Ur-r..uh. "Your word is a lamp to my feet, and a light to my path." (*points to his feet*)

EMILY: Good Ethan. (***EMILY** claps and starts to exit*) We need the light of God's Word wherever we walk each day. (*holding Bible*)

ETHAN: (*looks at **EMILY** oddly*) …or night

EMILY: …and night, you're right!

ETHAN: I won. (*throws hands up*)

EMILY: Well, you must have more in that head of yours than stuffing.

ETHAN: NOW I know it's time to say Good-bye.

EMILY: Bye, boys and girls. Try to learn a verse that will help you this week.

(**EMILY** *exits*)

ETHAN: Bye, everybody.

* * *

(*All scripture was taken from Psalm 119:2, 9-11, 16, 105, paraphrased.*)

"Falling Short" # 18.

THEME: God's standard based on Romans 3:22-24.

SUMMARY: Every person falls short of God's standard and needs to realize God sent His Son to bring salvation and forgiveness of sins to obtain God's acceptance. This skit can be used for Christmas, or Thomas Edison's birthday *(February 11)*.

CHARACTERS: *(two puppets seven to nine years old)*

    ROBBIE...*a boy who feels he is a failure*

    KATIE.....*a girl, his sympathetic sister*

(**ROBBIE** *enters with head down; tears in his eyes; hear sniffing*)

KATIE: What's wrong Robbie?

ROBBIE: I can't do anything right. *(sniff, sniff)* Nothing I do ever works out.

KATIE: Oh…what went wrong this time?

ROBBIE: We had our last baseball game of the season and I struck out. *(sobbing)*

KATIE: Is that all?

ROBBIE: That's a lot when it was the last inning and I was the last batter. (*sniffing*)

KATIE: So that ended the game, right?

ROBBIE: Right! (*still sniffing*) I let my team mates down.

KATIE: Robbie, you know you're not the only one that ever struck out.

ROBBIE: Well, I'm the only one who failed my team.

KATIE: No, I'm sure you're not. Some of your other team mates have felt the same way. Everyone struck out sometime.

ROBBIE: (*still sniffing*) No, they always get a hit.

KATIE: Somebody has to get an out, or the other team would never get up to bat. Everybody knows Michael Jordan, that great sports guy. I read in a book that he was cut from a team once, because he wasn't such a good player when he was young.

ROBBIE: No..o..o! You're kidding! *(pause)* I didn't know that.

KATIE: I'm sure he felt like a failure. But look at the player he became.

ROBBIE: Oh! He must have worked hard to overcome that failure.

KATIE: He sure did! *(pause)* Sometimes a failure makes us work harder and we accomplish a lot more than we would have otherwise.

ROBBIE: (*says in self-pity moaning tone*) Well, that won't happen to me.

KATIE: You've heard of Thomas Edison, the great inventor?

ROBBIE: What happened to him?

KATIE: His teacher thought he was stupid because he asked too many questions. His mother decided to take him out of school and try to answer his questions herself.

ROBBIE: Didn't she find another school for him?

KATIE: In the 1850's there weren't many schools and most kids didn't get to go to school at all; so she homeschooled him.

ROBBIE: I wonder if Thomas Edison ever got over asking so many questions.

KATIE: He certainly didn't stop thinking up new ideas. He invented the basics for electric lights, the phonograph, moving pictures, and other machines we use in our homes and offices today.

ROBBIE: What a smart guy!

KATIE: I read in a book that he tried and tried to find the right wire thread to keep the electric bulb lighted. Over and over he failed, but he kept thinking and trying to get a thread that wouldn't burn up.

ROBBIE: So he failed with his teacher at school, but he didn't cry and give up.

KATIE: You see, he learned from his failures and turned out to be one of the world's most brilliant inventors.

ROBBIE: I guess I had better stop fretting and get to work on a new plan.

KATIE: Sounds like a good idea. You know we have all failed in God's eyes. Romans 3:23 says everyone has sinned and comes short of what God wants.

ROBBIE: You mean God sees us all as failures?

KATIE: That's right. Everyone falls short of God's standard.

ROBBIE: I guess that means the earth is full of failing people.

KATIE: Yep, but they don't have to stay failures. God provided a way to succeed.

ROBBIE: Oh! How can you be so sure of that?

KATIE: When we come to realize we are sinners, we can ask God's forgiveness. He made a way of forgiveness through Jesus, his Son.

ROBBIE: Tell me more about God's way.

KATIE: You know we celebrate Jesus birth at Christmas. Jesus lived on earth thirty-three years as the only perfect person. Many people rejected what he said and did, but he didn't fail in carrying out God's plan.

ROBBIE: He didn't fail in God's plan?.. I thought Jesus was crucified.

KATIE: That's right. He died on the cross, was buried, but He rose again in three days as God planned He would. Then over 500 people saw Him before He went back to Heaven where God the Father rejoiced in His success.

ROBBIE: People saw Him alive, so did they believe in Him?

KATIE: Some did, and some didn't. It's the same today; eventhough we have all this recorded in the Bible. Some people still choose not to believe the Bible. Those people will always fall short of God's plan for them.

ROBBIE: I'm beginning to understand. We can choose to live as a sinful failure or we can let God change our life for his glory.

KATIE: That's right. Now, dry your tears and wash your face. You have a lot to look forward to when you know Jesus as your Savior.

ROBBIE: I'm glad God won't see me as a failure now that I have Jesus as my Savior.

KATIE: God not only gives us a better life here on earth, but gives us the hope of eternal life in heaven.

ROBBIE: WOW! I've got to get out of here and tell this important news to all the kids on my ball team. (***ROBBIE** leaves quickly.*)

KATIE: *(talks to the class before leaving)* I'm sure some of you boys and girls have had feelings of failing. Right? *(pause)* Aren't you glad we don't have to go around feeling like a failure? God can help us be a success if we trust him. Don't you want to make that change today?

* * *

(Other teachers can be prepared to talk to any pupils with questions.)

Bibliography:

"The Wizard of Menlo Park", *Inventor Stamp Book*, Sam L. Gabriel & Sons, NY.

"Thomas Alva Edison" *The World Book Encyclopedia*, Volume E.

"A Memory Poem" # 19.

THEME: Patriotism and Appreciation of Freedoms.

SUMMARY: Two girls talk about how important it is to remember those who fought for our freedom and how we can be patriotic and show appreciation for our freedoms.

CHARACTERS: *(two girl puppets ages 7 to 10)*

    MADIE.....*older girl puppet*

    GRACIE...*younger girl puppet*

SETTING: *In the family room*

PROPS: *Ball, pencil, paper, music and words to "America"*

*(**MADIE** is trying to write a poem. **GRACIE** enters bouncing her ball. Hear bouncing).*

GRACIE: What are you doing over there?

MADIE: Writing a memory story. Do you want something?

GRACIE: I want you to play ball with me.

MADIE: It's too hot. Why would I want to get all sweaty?

GRACIE: I want to play ball with you. Isn't that a good enough reason?

The Right Connection by Iris Gray Dowling

MADIE: Maybe for you, but not for me.

GRACIE: What is more important than having fun with a friend?

MADIE: I'm writing down my memory story.

GRACIE: You're what?

MADIE: Writing a memorial day *pome*. (*poem*)

GRACIE: What's a pome?

MADIE: A rhyme, silly!

GRACIE: You mean a po-em!

MADIE: Yeah, a poem to remember those who gave everything so we could have lots of freedoms.

GRACIE: Lot's of men and women did that!

MADIE: I was just thinking of the soldiers serving our country now. We owe them a lot, but there are so many we can't say thank you to all of them.

GRACIE: You're right. Think of all the years in our history. There must have been millions who fought to make our country free.

MADIE: A long time ago when George Washington was alive, he fought as a soldier in several wars. He did a lot as a soldier and great leader to help us live in a free country. He led a lot of other people to do the same.

GRACIE: Oh, but that was a real long time ago.

MADIE: Probably more than 250 years ago, but if no one had cared back then, we wouldn't have a free country today.

GRACIE: I never thought of it that way.

MADIE: When we have patriotic holidays, we all need to remember the people from our country's past who cared enough to fight and take a stand when it was necessary.

GRACIE: Maybe more than on patriotic holidays; we should remember them all the time.

MADIE: You're right, Gracie. We have to be thankful for the freedoms we have all the time. That's why I was writing a poem today.

GRACIE: I guess we do need to show we are thankful. Another way is to sing a patriotic or thankful song. Do you know any?

MADIE: How about if we sing "My Country Tis of Thee". Then I'll read my poem.

*[Both **GIRLS** sing "America" together. Audience can join in singing.]*

MADIE: (*reads her poem*)
"There were many who fought and died,
They never knew what it was to really be free;
But I'm thankful they cared enough to give what they had
To make a free country for you and for me."

The Right Connection by Iris Gray Dowling

GRACIE: I'm glad you wrote that poem. It tells exactly how we should feel about those who gave so much. Now let's go out to play ball.

MADIE: Wait, Gracie. Just singing and writing a poem are only two small ways to show we're thankful.

GRACIE: What else?

MADIE: By using our freedoms…going to church when the doors are open…or being proud to read the Bible anywhere.

GRACIE: Yes, I agree, but my parents don't take me to church.

MADIE: Another thing is to not be ashamed to pray in public.

GRACIE: Isn't that the preacher's job?

MADIE: No, I mean in restaurants or the cafeteria before we eat. We also need to pray about the problems we have when our friends see us.

GRACIE: Why do we need to do that?

MADIE: It shows we aren't afraid to use our freedom of speech. I often hear Dad say "use it or lose it."

GRACIE: I didn't think of it that way.

MADIE: If we don't use our freedoms, we will never know how important they are until we lose them.

GRACIE: That wouldn't make a good memory, would it?

MADIE: No, way!

GRACIE: I'm glad we had this talk and you wrote that poem. I'm glad I can be free to play ball if I want.

MADIE: All right, let's go play ball now. (*Both exit*)

* * *

The Right Connection by Iris Gray Dowling

20.   "Something Different to Surprise Dad"

SUMMARY: Jenna wants to make Dad's day memorable. She can't think of a different surprise. She asked her friend, Ben, but finally got an unusual idea from her little sister, Katie.

CHARACTERS: *(three puppets)*

    JENNA.....*ten year old girl*

    BEN.........*Jenna's friend, has party hat on his head*

    KATIE.....*five-year old little sister*

PROPS: *laptop, paper, crayons, card, bowl, party hat*

JENNA: Sunday is Father's Day. What can I do that's special for Dad? *[pause]* Let me see, I can get a card, *(pause)* but I've never liked those stick figure ones. It's hard to get a card for a man like Dad. He doesn't like flowers or odd-looking bottles on his card.

BEN: *(wearing a pointed party hat)* Hi, Jenna. It looks like you have a big problem.

JENNA: I don't know what to do for my Dad this Father's Day.

BEN: That's not hard. Get a card.

JENNA: I want to do something different. Most cards cost too much and don't look worth a dime.

BEN: Then make one on your computer.

JENNA: I thought of that, but I did that last year. I wanted to do something really different.

BEN: Oh, I guess I'm not much help. Do you think he'd like the perfume you're wearing? *(motions like leaving)*

JENNA: Of course not! Men wear shaving lotion.

BEN: Why don't you get him shaving lotion then?

JENNA: That's a good idea. Thanks, Ben. But I still feel like I need to think of something better.

BEN: Well let me get my thinking cap on straight.

JENNA: It looks like you have it on straight.

BEN: Oh! It hasn't been very helpful, has it?

JENNA: Take it off then and help me get another GOOD idea.

BEN: Okay. *(pause)* Maybe you could do a chore for your dad.

JENNA: What kind of chore could I do?

BEN: Let him choose. You just tell him you'll work for two hours as a gift.

The Right Connection by Iris Gray Dowling

JENNA: Oh, that's a great idea! He'll love that! I'll make a card and add a note about my gift.

BEN: Guess what? I like the idea so well I'm going home and do the same for my Dad. See you later. (***BEN*** *leaves*)

(***JENNA*** *gets her laptop to make the card*)

KATIE: (*little sister enters*) What are you doing, Jenna?

JENNA: I'm making something for Father's Day.

KATIE: I want to help.

JENNA: You can't do what I'm planning, Katie.

KATIE: Why not? I wanted to make a cake, but Mommy said I'm too little. I want to help with a card and you say I'm too little, too. When will I ever get big enough?

JENNA: Oh, Katie, you just gave me an even better idea. I'll help you make a cake and you can help me make the card and we'll share in giving them to Dad.

KATIE: Why don't we make a cake and decorate it to look like a card?

JENNA: Wow, Katie! That's an awesome idea! That's exactly what we'll do. You're so smart!

KATIE: Can I help put the icing on the cake?

JENNA: Yes, you ice the first layer and I'll put the second layer on and ice it. Then you can lick the spoon and clean the bowl.

KATIE: I can't wait to taste that icing.

JENNA: Okay. While you enjoy the icing, I'll make the cake look like a card. I'll make some blue icing and write: "Happy Father's Day, DAD…We love YOU…Jenna and Katie."

KATIE: Maybe you could put a big heart at the top and two little ones by our names.

JENNA: This will be the best Father's Day our Dad has ever had! Let's get to work, so we'll be ready by tomorrow.

KATIE: Okay. What can I do?

JENNA: You work on making a paper card while I get the ingredients for the cake. Be sure to make the same design on the card as we'll put on the cake. I'll add the message about doing chores on the inside of our card.

KATIE: *(gives JENNA a hug)* Thanks, Jenna. I love you for letting me help with Dad's present.

JENNA: Your help was just what I needed.

(Puppets Exit)

* * *

God's Plan: **From the Manger to the Cross**

Other Sources for Puppet Skits Written by Iris Gray Dowling

I. Rights owned by these Publishers. Contact the Publisher.

Puppet titles in <u>Upward Bound,</u> Contact Eldridge Plays & Musicals. Venice, FL 34284

    1. "Major Decision" –making a decision to accept Jesus gift of Salvation.

    2. "Light At the End of the Tunnel" – how God used Joseph to save his people.

    3. "Be Careful What You Hear" – learning to please God with every part of our life.

    4. "Shawn's Missionary Work" – Shawn earns money for a mission project.

    5. "Lost and Found" – Doug lost his friend and accidentally found a new friend.

    6. "The Important Birthday Presents" – learning the second birthday is more important.

    7. "A Wise Decision" – Matthew 7:24-29—building on the right foundation.

    8. "The Journey Home" –Onesimus returns to his master for forgiveness.

9. "Life's Connection – In John 3 Nicodemus learns what it means to be born again.

10. "A Coward—Not Me" – showing that being prejudiced is not Christ like.

11. "The Special Christmas Light" – tells the purpose and meaning of the Christmas Star.

* * * * * * * * *

Four Puppet titles by Iris Dowling were published by *One Way Street Inc.,* a supplier of puppets, scripts, and other puppet ministry resources. Contact *One Way Street* at 11999 East Caley Avenue, Centennial, CO 80111 (Phone: 303.790.1188) www.onewaystreet.com.

1. "Turning Over a New Leaf" – The puppets realize God gives us many new things to look forward to. Published 1-1998.

2. "Leap Year Birthday" – Renee is not upset that she was born physically on February 29 because she has a spiritual birthday every year. Pub.-2-1998.

3. "The Cover Up" – Josie puts band aids on his chicken pox like some people try to cover up their sins. Published 5-2002

4. "Battle Strategies" – As a good soldier George Washington set the example for a Christian soldier. Based on Ephesians 6. Published 6-2003.

* * * * * * * * *

Puppet titles written by Iris Dowling and published by *National Drama Service* (contact *Life Way Church Resources),* Southern Baptist Convention. (Phone: 615.251.3771)

1. "April First Birthday" – an April Fool's joke becomes an inspirational thought. NDS-Volume 11, #2, Spring 2003, page 37.

2. "Leftovers" – At Thanksgiving children learn to give God their best, not their leftovers. NDS-Volume 7, #4, Fall 1999, page 5.

3. "The Path of Truth" – George Washington emphasizes the importance of reading the Bible to children. NDS-Volume 7, #1, Winter 1998-99, page 35.

4. "God's Trumpets" – Joshua's obedience at the Battle of Jericho. NDS-Volume 6, #3, Summer 1998, page 42.

5. "Wearing An Honest Man's Hat" – looking up to Abe Lincoln for honesty. NDS-Volume 5, #1, Winter 1997-98, page 35.

6. "Bible Translators" – how the Bible was translated in New Guinea. NDS-Volume 6, #1, Winter 1997-98, page 31.

7. "Something Different for Mother" – giving Mom a special gift.NDS-Volume 3, #2, Apr/May 1995, page 7.

8. "Second Sight" – God made each person for the purpose of pleasing Him.. NDS-Fall-1995, Sunday school Board of SBC.

* * * * * * * * *

Puppet Titles published by *Creatively Yours Puppetry*, 1737 W. 37th Plaza, Tulsa, OK 74132 (Phone: 918.446.2424)

1. "Thanks For Dad" – Jeff comes to realize what a great Dad he has. Sold 4-1995. *CYP.*

2. "The Stolen Radio"– a child saves money to buy radios for mission work. 1993. *CYP.*

* * * * * * * * * *

Puppet Title published by *Shining Star Magazine*. Frank Schaeffer Publication.

1. "Freedom's Shore"-- See God's plan for a land of freedom. Volume 57., F. Schaeffer. Published 8-1999. Used by permission.

* * * * * * * * * *

II.. Puppet Skits-- Rights owned by Iris Dowling. You may contact the Author:

Puppet Titles published by *Standard Publishing Company*, Hamilton, Ohio.

1. "The Wise Builder"– Building life on the right foundation; Father's Day, 2003.

2. "Real Love Came Down" – Valentine's Day--showing Jesus has real love. *Programs for Special Days,* Standard Publishing, 1999, page 4, and also in *School & Church Programs for the Whole Year,* Masthof Press, 2006, page 31.

3. "Hope Is in the Lord" – Chung and Alex learn friendship. *Programs for Special Days*, page 34.

    *   *   *   *   *   *   *   *   *   *

III. Books by Iris Gray Dowling that contain puppet skits: (Owned by author)

Christmas Program Ideas, 2005. Faithful Life Publishers, (84 pages)

 1. "Remember God's Gifts"—Alicia learns about the most important gift. page 58.

School and Church Program Ideas for the Whole Year, 2006. Masthof Publisher. Permission granted by the author. (218 pages)

 1. "I'll Go Wherever He Sends Me"-- Phillip and the Eunuch, Acts 8. page 55.

 2. "Freedom's Shore" -- God's plan for a land of freedom. page 8.

 3. "Mystery Visitor" – Lincoln appears for his birthday. page 23.

 4. "Real Love Came Down"—Jesus brought everlasting love. page 31.

 5. "Here Am I Send Me"—accepting the missionary call. First in *ABWE Mission Magazine*. page 43 in *School and Church Program Ideas*.

6. "My Family Cares"—Jason learns his family can help. page 133.

7. "Growing in God's Garden"—learning from Grandpa's garden. page 159.

Declare His Name, ABWE Publishing, 2001 (4 Mission skits by IGD.)

1. "The Turning Point"—story of reaching the Auca Indians. page 69.

2. "Invisible Rewards"—children learn the value of sharing their home with visiting missionaries. page 77.

3. "Whom Shall I Send?"—MK's and friends talk about having to leave their home for foreign mission work. page 85.

4. "Our Hope is in the Lord"—a new Chinese boy tells about his friend--Jesus. page 91.

* * * * * * * * * *

Inquire or order (if available) from the author by E-mail:

~~irisgdow@juno.com~~

dowlingiris013@gmail.com

Topical Index for "The Right Connection" (Puppet Skits)

(This Index may help if you are looking for a skit about a certain Biblical character, reference or topic. (Numbers of the skits 1-20)

Biblical Characters and References: (# of skit)

Noah -- Genesis 7– 9	#1, 2
David -- 1 Samuel 16, 17	#16
Daniel -- Daniel 6	#5, 6, 8
Nebuchadnezzar—Daniel 4	#5
Belshazzar—Daniel 5	#6
Jonah – Jonah 1--3	#3
Jesus – Philippians 2:10,	#5
Blind Man – John 9	#14
Paul and Philemon	#15
Onesimus -- Philemon 1	#15

Biblical References and Topics found in the Puppet skits.

1 Samuel 16:7	#9
Psalms 119:2, 9-11, 105	#7, 17
Matthew 5:13-16	#11
John 14:1-6	#12, 13
John 3:16	#1, 10, 14, 18
Romans 3:22-24; 6:23	#1, 14, #11, 18
Colossians 4:7-9	#15
Hebrews 11:7	#1, 10, 14, 18
1 Peter 3:3-5	#11
Revelation 20:15; 21:27	#12, 13

(continued on next page)

The Right Connection by Iris Gray Dowling

Bible Study	#7, 17
Birthdays (Dad)	#20
Blindness	#14
Christmas	#18
Easter	#18
Edison, Thomas	#18
Forgiveness	#9, 15, 18
Heaven	#12, 13
Heroes	#11
History	#5, 6
Missions	#8
Obedience	#3
Patriotism	#9, 19
Prayer	#6, 8
Pride	#5, 6, 7, 9
Salvation	#1, 14, 18
Saving the Earth	#12
Sports	#11, 16
Stealing	#8, 15
Trusting	#2, 16
Washington, George	#19

Brief Bio of the Author

Iris Gray Dowling, a Southeastern Pennsylvania freelance writer, has been active in Elementary education for over 50 years (25+ in public schools, 25+ as homeschool advisor, 45 years as a Junior Church teacher, as well as Vacation Bible School, Sunday school, and other children's clubs.) Iris has a B.S. and M. Ed. from West Chester University. Her travels in the U.S. and overseas inspired the settings for some of her writing.

Iris has published more than 1500 poems, puppet skits, short plays, church programs, fiction and nonfiction stories, teaching articles, and puzzles in a variety of publications. It is her desire to encourage others to submit their talents to the Lord and watch what He can do through them. (Philippians 4:13).

Here are some books written by Iris Gray Dowling.
(Sales made by e-mail).

- *Echoing Memories* – Stories with Read and Think Skills

- *Nature Stories with a Twist* – Science Stories with a Biblical Devotion.

- *History of Churches and Worship Groups in the Oxford Area,* (PA.)

- *A Change of Hats* – Picture Book for Kindergarten and Preschool ages.

- *A Pony for my Birthday* – Easy Reader for Grades 1 to 4.

- *Mission Journeys from Upper Oxford Township, PA.* – Mission stories.

- *School and Church Program Ideas for the Whole Year* – poems, plays.

- *Christmas Program Ideas*--poems, exercises, and plays.

- *Upward Bound, Volume #1* – 11 puppet skits for children.

- *The Right Connection* – 20 more puppet skits for children.

- *Declare His Name* – mission dramas for mission conferences.

- *Through the Eye-Gate* – 52 object lesson ideas.